Quantifying IT Stability

Dominique A. Heger Ph.D.

iUniverse, Inc.
New York   Bloomington

Quantifying IT Stability

iUniverse books may be ordered through booksellers or by contacting:

iUniverse
1663 Liberty Drive
Bloomington, IN 47403
www.iuniverse.com
1-800-Authors (1-800-288-4677)

ISBN: 978-1-4401-0697-2 (pbk)
ISBN: 978-1-4401-0698-9 (ebk)

Printed in the United States of America

iUniverse rev. date:12/12/08

About the Author

Dominique A. Heger has over 20 years of IT experience, focusing on systems performance, capacity planning, cluster technology, performance modeling, algorithms and data structures, and I/O scalability. He worked for IBM, Hewlett-Packard, and Unisys. Over the years, he published over 30 papers with CMG, IEEE, or IBM Press on systems performance related topics, and authored 3 core chapters of the *Performance Tuning for Linux Servers* book that was released in 2005. He holds a Ph.D. in Information Systems from NSU, Florida. He is the owner and founder of DHTechnologies (www.dhtusa.com), an IT consulting company in Austin, TX.

Table of Contents

About the Author..v

Preface.. xiii

Acknowledgements...xv

Introduction... xvii

Chapter 1 - Grid Technology – Vision, Architecture, & Terminology 1

    Introduction..1

    Virtualization of Computing Resources...2

    Types of Grid Environments 3

    Grid Layers 5

    Grid Applications 8

    Globus Grid Toolkit 9

    Summary - Benefits of Grid computing 11

    References 13

Chapter 2 - Parallel Systems & File System Technologies in a Cluster Environment 15

    Introduction..15

    Parallel Systems 16

    Parallel Architectures 17

    Communication and Memory Architecture Models 18

    Parallel Application Performance 19

    Programming Models and Methods..20

    Performance Metrics for Communication Mechanisms 21

    Shared Memory Architectures 22

    Cache Coherent Uniform Memory Access Architecture 23

    Massively Parallel Processing Architecture...24

    Replicated Memory Cluster Architecture 25

    Cache Coherent Non Uniform Memory Access Architecture....................25

    Non Cache Coherent Non Uniform Memory Access Architecture............27

    Cache Only Memory Access Architecture 27

    Distributed Virtual Shared Memory Architecture 28

    Simple Cache Only Memory Access Architecture....................................29

    Cluster File Systems and Cluster Applications...31

    Cluster File System Terminology 32

    Introduction to IBM' General Parallel File System (GPFS)......................34

    Red Hat's Global File System (GFS)..36

    GFS Version 3 37

    GFS Version 4 38

GFS Version 6 - Internals...44
GFS Version 6 - Layout 45
GFS Version 6 – Scalability & Availability Considerations 46
GFS Version 6 - Backup Capabilities 47
Summary and Conclusion 48
References...49
Chapter 3 – InfiniBand, SAN and NAS – Introduction, Performance, & Technology 53
Introduction..53
InfiniBand - Definition...53
InfiniBand – Usage & Application...54
SAN & NAS Solutions 56
NAS Terminology 58
SAN Terminology 59
SAN & Fibre Channel...60
Summary 61
References...62
Chapter 4 - A Cohesive Framework to Quantify Computer Systems Assurance..............65
Introduction..65
The CSA Equation 65
CSA – Product Assurance 67
Reliability Dimension 68
Maintainability Dimension 68
Availability Dimension 68
CSA - Dependability 69
Security Dimension...69
Safety Dimension..70
CSA – Performability/Scalability 70
CSA – Methodology & Case Study 71
Summary 75
References...76
Chapter 5 - Modeling Based Performance Engineering 79
Introduction..79
Performance Design Considerations..79
Performance Modeling..80
Where to Start 82
Methodology to Conduct End-to-End Performance Analysis 83
Summary 86
References...88
Chapter 6 - Reliability Engineering - Business Aspects, Concepts, and Tools.................89

Introduction...89
Reliability Engineering Concepts 89
Failure Mode and Effects Analysis (FMEA) 91
Summary..95
References..96
Chapter 7 - Maintenance Systems...97
Introduction...97
Maintenance Conditions 97
Maintenance Processes 98
Business Aspects..100
Maintenance Systems Control 101
Effect of Condition Monitoring on Maintenance Systems 101
Summary 102
References...104
Chapter 8 - Using Statistical Data to Analyze Reliability & to Schedule Maintenance ..105
Introduction...105
Censored Versus Complete Data..105
Weibull distribution...106
Maximum Likelihood Estimation 109
Moment estimation 109
Probability Plotting & Hazard Plotting......................................109
Preventive Maintenance 110
The Interrelationship among Reliability, Availability, and Maintainability.............112
Summary 114
References...115
Chapter 9 - Evaluating Systems Stability and the Dynamics of Large Transients 117
Introduction...117
Metastability 118
Microscopic Metastability 118
Macroscopic Metastability...119
Transition Dynamics in a VLAN 120
Quantification of the Transition Time 123
Summary 127
References...128
Chapter 10 - A Workload-Dependent Scalability Model for Parallel Applications 131
Introduction...131
Parallel Application Performance 132
Programming Models and Methods..133
Speedup Function...134

The Factorized Scaleup Function...135
Serialization Issues on Parallel Systems 137
Coherency Issues on Parallel Systems..138
I/O Scaleup Analysis on an MPP System 139
(Non-linear) Regression Analysis 141
I/O Scaleup Analysis on an SMP System 143
NAS Scaleup Analysis on a Linux Cluster 145
Summary 146
References 148
Chapter 11 - Deterministic Stochastic Petri Net I/O Performance Quantification 151
Introduction...151
Deterministic Stochastic Petri Nets 152
Linux 2.6 I/O Stack & RAID Subsystems 154
The Deadline I/O Scheduler 156
The Anticipatory I/O scheduler 157
The CFQ Scheduler...158
The Noop I/O scheduler...158
Modeled I/O Stack 159
DSPN Model 160
Simulation Experiments and Analysis 161
Summary 165
References 167
Chapter 12 - Quantitative Disk I/O Capacity Performance 171
Introduction...171
Contemporary Disk Technology 172
Performance Implications 173
Disk Capacity & I/O Throughput Model 175
Capacity Model Calibration & Validation 178
Summary 180
References 182
Chapter 13 - An Introduction to Operations Research..185
Introduction...185
OR Activities...185
OR Functions and Methods 186
OR in Manufacturing 187
Production Systems..188
Time Series Analysis...191
Forecasting 192
Statistical methods 192

Summary 194
References 195
Index 197

Preface

What is the Grid? As the World Wide Web is a service for sharing information over the Internet, the Grid is a service for sharing computer power and data storage capacity over the Internet. The Grid goes well beyond simple communication between computers, and aims ultimately to turn the global network of computers into one vast computational resource. It has to be pointed out though that this is the dream, the ultimate goal. Reality today is that the Grid is a work in progress, with the underlying technology still in a semi-prototype phase, and being developed by hundreds of researchers and software engineers around the globe. The Grid is attracting a lot of interest, as its future, despite being uncertain right now, is potentially not just evolutionary, but actually revolutionary. In a nutshell, the interest comes not only from experts in computer science, but from scientists in other fields, commercial businesses, government agencies, or the stock market.

Lets imagine several million computer systems, ranging from laptops to clusters. Let's further imagine that these systems are situated all over the globe. Obviously, they belong to different people and institutions. This picture is actually nothing new, as this is pretty much what the IT world looks like today. Now lets imagine that all these systems are connected to the Internet. Still not much new here, most of them are probably connected already. Now imagine that you have a magic tool, which makes all of them act as a single, vast and powerful computer system. That picture now is really is different. This huge, sprawling interconnect of computer systems that are spread over the globe is what the Grid is supposed to represent. As anybody in IT knows, it is hard enough to keep large symmetric multi-processor (SMP) or small cluster based systems up and running. A lot of companies around the globe do not have a great grip on reliability, availability, maintainability, or scalability (the system stability components) on a small scale. Hence, the question at hand is how are these issues being addressed (and understood) on large cluster systems or even the Grid? How are these terms interrelated, and how do IT personnel quantify them in an efficient and effective manner? Are system stability issues encountered on the Grid building block (the individual nodes) the final stumbling block in the evolution of the Grid? Are we today really addressing these issues or are we just masking the symptoms?

Frankly, I do have oversimplified this to make a point. The real world is even more confusing than what I have described here; as security related issues have a profound impact on the Grid nodes as well. While writing this book, my focus was on highlighting the systems stability components and to provide the reader with the basic knowledge and skills needed to understand the interrelationships among these terms. This will allow the reader to design, architecture, evaluate, and deploy small and large IT systems with a high degree of customer satisfaction. This book also allows the reader to better understand the key technologies behind cluster systems and the Grid, allowing for a smother transition (where applicable) from SMP based environments into the cluster and Grid arena.

Acknowledgements

This book is dedicated to anybody who has spent countless hours addressing reliability, availability, maintainability, scalability, and security issues on ill-designed IT systems. This book has been a work in progress for several years, and hence I would like to thank all my friends and co-workers at Hewlett-Packard and IBM for their support, guidance, and input. A special shout-out goes to my wife Karin, thanks much for all your love and support.

All the trademarks mentioned in this book are the property of the respective companies. No warranties are made, express or implied that the information in this book is error free or that they will meet the requirements for any particular system. The author disclaims all liability for direct or consequential damages resulting from the use of this book.

Introduction

This book presents a unique perspective on how terms such as GRID, cluster, parallel file system, reliability, availability, maintainability, and scalability are interrelated and how to quantify overall system stability in ever larger system environments that today may span around the globe.

The term *GRID* is increasingly appearing in the computer literature, generally referring to some form of system framework into which hardware, software, or information resources can be plugged, and which permits easy configuration and creation of new functionality from existing resources. The applications for these grid concepts include computational challenge problems requiring supercomputing capabilities, universal availability of customized computing services, and global integration of information, computing, and other resources for various purposes. The building blocks for these GRID systems are in a lot of cases individual cluster systems that are interconnected to increase the processing range. Data storage and movement are of increasing importance to the Grid. Over time, scientific and commercial applications have evolved to process larger volumes of data, and thus their overall throughput is inextricably tied to the timely delivery of data. As the usage of the Grid evolves to include more and more commercial applications, data management will likely become even more central than it is today. While performance has long been the focus of GRID, cluster, server, and storage systems alike, recent trends indicate that other factors, such as scalability, reliability, availability, and manageability, may now be more relevant and mission critical. The argument made is that manageability has become the dominant criterion in evaluating IT solutions. To illustrate, the cost of storage management outweighs the cost of the storage devices themselves by a factor of three to eight.

This book introduces the reader to the concepts, architectures, philosophies, and methodologies behind terms such as GRID, cluster, SAN, NAS, IO storage, or interconnect. While these terms appear in the literature on a regular basis, this book takes a unique approach, as it focuses on quantifying scalability, reliability, availability, and maintainability issues surrounding these rather large IT environments. The goal of this book is to illustrate how they are all linked together and hence how they have to be analyzed and quantified as a unit. While the scope of the presented material is diverse, my intention was to cover all the basic elements first that are necessary to build a sound IT foundation, and second to put the pieces together to complete the puzzle.

The book uses a simple, pragmatic, and progressive approach to discussing the importance of understanding the interrelationships among reliability, availability, maintainability, scalability, and security in small and large IT environments. The first part of the book is focused on introducing the Grid, cluster systems and their main building blocks like parallel file systems, IO storage, SAN and NAS environments, or high-speed interconnects. The second part of the book elaborates on a methodology that allows IT architects and designers to better understand and quantify the above discussed interrelationships common in an IT environment. Throughout the book, simple mathematical and analytical models are used to quantify systems stability components. The last part of the book consists of several case studies that allow the reader to further understand the complexity issues encountered in the real world.

The individual chapters in this book are organized as following. Chapter 1 elaborates on the GRID architecture, terminology, vision, and implementation. Further, the chapter discusses what kinds of applications are suitable for a GRID environment. Chapter 2 introduces in a more in-depth manner cluster technologies and parallel file systems. These components are considered major building blocks for GRID systems. Chapter 3 highlights some of the advanced interconnect technologies available to inter-link nodes and IO subsystem components, respectively. The chapter further elaborates on the similarities and differences between SAN and NAS implementations. Chapter 4 introduces the Cohesive Systems Insurance (CSA) methodology that is proposed in this book to quantify the aggregate stability of an IT infrastructure. Chapter 5 discusses some of the performance engineering (PE) methodologies available to systems and application design and implementation specialists. More specifically, the chapter discusses the importance of building performance into the final solution, a process that has to start early in the design phase. Chapter 6 elaborates on reliability engineering, discussing the business aspects, concepts, and tools. The chapter introduces the failure mode and affects analysis (FMEA) and outlines how to best utilize the methodologies. In chapter 7, maintenance activities are discussed from a systemic point of view. Maintenance is considered from the selected viewpoint as a control system for controlling the reliability of machines in a process environment. Chapter 8 discusses why maintenance scheduling or reliability studies do not have to be based solely on an expert opinion. By carefully recording failure data, or using failure data from manufacturers, maintenance schedules and reliability studies can be economically optimized by utilizing statistical methods. Chapter 9 utilizes a case study to quantify the systems stability and the dynamics of large transients. Chapter 10 introduces a workload dependent scalability model for parallel applications. The model can be used in the design and the systems evaluation phases, respectively. Chapter 11 discusses how a deterministic stochastic Petri net model can be utilized to quantify IO performance, whereas chapter 12 utilizes an analytical model to determine the quantitative capacity of an IO subsystem. Chapter 13 introduces operations research (OR) and discusses OR's relationship to IT.

Chapter 1 - Grid Technology – Vision, Architecture, & Terminology

Introduction

In today's economic environment, any organization aims at reducing the time-to-market as well as any associated cost factors. At the same time, constraints on processing power, and the limitations on existing computing infrastructures hamper the implementation of efficient and effective IT solutions. It is increasingly important today to explore new avenues to utilize the existing IT resources. In many industries (such as financial services, manufacturing, or life sciences), significant improvements to the bottom line have been realized by adopting some form of Grid computing. The basic idea behind Grid computing is to interconnect (and utilize) available processor, storage, and memory sub-components of distributed computing systems to solve larger problems more efficiently. The benefits of Grid computing are (1) cost savings, (2) improved business agility by decreasing the time-to-market (delivering actual results), and (3) enhanced collaboration and sharing of resources among departments or institutions.

The basic concept of Grid networking is not new, what *is* relatively new is the current transition of Grid networking from R&D into the commercial market. This chapter introduces the vision of Grid networking, and the rather pragmatic evolution that was taken to realize that vision. The chapter elaborates on the Grid architecture and technologies that surround the Grid paradigm. Further, this chapter addresses some of the issues surrounding Grid applications. To reiterate, the vision of the Grid movement is to virtualize the computing landscape, focusing on the main goal of creating an actual *utility computing model* that is distributed over a set of resources. In general, a single compute node includes some basic elements such as processors, some storage (I/O) subsystem, an operating system, and some form of network/interconnect interface. The basic concept of Grid computing is to establish a similar environment, over a distributed area, incorporating heterogeneous elements such as server nodes, storage devices, and network components in a scaleable, wide-area spanning compute infrastructure. The software that coordinates the participating components and elements is analogous to the operating system in a single compute or server environment.

Virtualization of Computing Resources

Virtualizing the compute resources yields a scaleable (and flexible) pool of processing and data storage components that can be utilized to improve efficiency. Moreover, it aims at generating a competitive advantage by streamlining product development, allowing an organization to focus on their core business. Over time, Grid environments will enable the creation of virtual organizations and advanced Web services, as partnerships and collaborations become more critical in strengthening each link in the value chain. It has to be pointed out though that nowadays there are many definitions for Grid computing, but the core concept revolves around the *"aggregation of geographically dispersed computing, storage, and network resources, coordinated to deliver improved performance, higher quality of service, better utilization, and easier access to data. It enables virtual, collaborative organizations, sharing applications and data in an open, heterogeneous environment"* [3].

The common denominator for all Grid deployments is the network layer. The shared network fabric is the component that connects all of the resources in a Grid, and hence has a profound impact on the success of a Grid implementation. Therefore, high-speed data networking technologies have been the cornerstone for the evolution of the Grid technology. Distributed Grid systems demand high-speed connectivity and provide very low latency behaviors. High-performance Ethernet switching elements are paramount in meeting these requirements. Hence, the statement can be made that components such as (bundled) Gigabit Ethernet interfaces or 10-Gigabit Ethernet connections are considered a necessity to achieve the performance goals [7]. Over time, as the Grid infrastructure evolves from cluster systems to (1) virtualized enterprise data centers to (2) large distributed, wide-area spanning deployments, the underlying network infrastructure has to grow in a cost-effective manner, be scaleable, and meet the performance requirements.

Grid computing evolved out of the academic research community and the national defense industry, where researchers have to process vast amounts of data as efficiently as possible (mostly in simulation related projects). Utilizing the original concept of Grid computing, arrays of computational power and storage are constructed from a network of many small (and sometimes widespread) compute nodes. The resulting infrastructure is used to perform large calculation and operation based studies, where the workload generator (application) can be decomposed into independent units of work. This approach allows massive computational projects to achieve results that otherwise could not be completed, even on today's largest super-computers. To re-emphasize, as the concept has evolved, Grid computing has gained some acceptance in the commercial marketplace. Institutions with both, large and small networks have adopted Grid techniques to (1) reduce the aggregate execution time, and (2) to enable resource sharing.

Types of Grid Environments

There are three basic types of Grid environments discussed in the industry today. (1) The compute Grid, (2) the data Grid, and the (3) utility Grid. On the other hand, from an application perspective, there are two types of Grid environments, the compute and the data Grids, respectively [1],[3]. From a topology perspective, the argument made is that there are additional Grid types, such as the cluster systems, intra-Grids, extra-Grids, and inter-Grids. In reality, clusters, intra-Grids, extra-Grids, and inter-Grids can be better defined as representing stages of the Grid evolution. In each of these stages, it is feasible to support compute Grids, data Grids, or a combination of both types. The majority of the early Grid deployments have focused on enhancing computation, but as data Grids provide easier access to large, shared data sets, data Grids are becoming increasingly important.

A *compute Grid* is essentially a collection of distributed computing resources (within one or multiple locations). The compute resources are aggregated to act as a unified processing resource (virtual super-computer). The process of interconnecting these resources into a unified pool involves the coordination of the usage policies, job scheduling, queuing issues, Grid security, as well as user authentication. The main benefit of a compute Grid is to construct an infrastructure that allows efficient processing of compute-intensive jobs, by utilizing existing resources.

A *data Grid* provides distributed, secure access to current data. Data Grids enable managing (and efficiently utilize) database information from distributed locations. Much like a compute Grid, data Grids also have to rely on software components to insure secure access and to enforce usage policies. Data Grids (as well as compute Grids) can be deployed within one or across multiple domains. Data Grids eliminate the necessity to move, replicate, or centralize data. Actual data Grids are being used today, primarily serving collaborative research communities [4].

The evolution from compute Grids to data Grids is an important factor in repositioning Grid applications from education and R&D to large, commercial enterprises. This transition is an indicator that the market (and the technology itself) is maturing. From a networking perspective, the impact of data Grids includes a tighter integration of storage protocols and high-performance networking. As the middle-ware components for Grid infrastructures mature, coupled with the recent advances in data networking equipment, the statement can be made that the necessary momentum for evolving Grids from local clusters to distributed, wide-area systems is well defined. The first stage of Grid computing revolves around clusters. Based on the true definition of a Grid that includes terms like *distributed and heterogeneous*, it is debatable whether cluster systems should actually be considered as a Grid solution. Semantics aside, nevertheless, clusters are paramount in the evolution of Grid computing. Clusters are often defined by using terms such as distributed or parallel file systems or by a collection of homogeneous server nodes that are aggregated for increased performance. Chapter 2 further discusses cluster technologies and parallel file system solutions. Cluster systems are largely being used in application domains such as simulation-based testing and evaluation. The majority of the newer cluster systems utilize high-speed interconnects such as bundled Gigabit Ethernet, Myrinet, InfiniBand, or any other (sometimes proprietary) high-throughput network interface. Low-latency switching elements are critical in maintaining application performance across the cluster fabric.

To reiterate, cluster systems are critical in the evolution of Grid computing. As in order to move to the next phase (*intra-Grids*), these cluster systems have to be interconnected. By interconnecting individual cluster systems, it is feasible to enable the establishment of enterprise and inter-departmental Grid systems. The creation of intra-Grids puts additional strain on the controlling software layer (middle-ware) and the underlying network infrastructure. The middle-ware has to have a better understanding of the resource allocation, based on the additional complexity of the processor-sharing relationships. Further, latency issues at the network layer become more challenging, shifting the focus to even higher throughput-capable interconnects. In a next phase, extra-Grids will reflect cluster or intra-Grids that are connected among geographically distributed sites within either a single or among several organizations. The two important distinctions made for an extra-Grid are (1) geographic distribution and (2) inter-enterprise relationships. Because of these relationships, extra-Grids are sometimes referred to as partner Grids. In such a partner Grid, as the data can be shared among different organizations, authentication, policy management, and security issues become even more critical, a fact that has to be addressed by the Grid middle-ware layer. Further, load balancing, topology discovery, network (LAN/WAN) throughput, and application awareness are other factors that have to be considered to provide adequate performance and stability.

The final stage in the evolution of Grid computing revolves around the *inter-Grid* paradigm. This stage reflects the most powerful phase of Grid evolution, as it embodies two of the primary visions for Grid computing, (1) the utility computing infrastructure and (2) the Grid services providers. Although this is the final stage (which has not yet been reached from a commercial perspective), it has to be pointed out that inter-Grids do exist today in the R&D domain (the TeraGrid as an example). Inter-Grid setups surpass all the other phases in regards to the relative complexity requirements. To illustrate this point, compared to a setup where a couple of institutions participate in an extra-Grid environment, an inter-Grid may service thousands of users. As a result, all of the complex requirements at the middle-ware and the network layer are increased significantly. Grid setups in this stage are also referred to as utility Grids. At this time, two significant statements about the status quo of Grid implementations can be made. (1) Cluster systems are evolving toward intra-Grid setups in the commercial world. (2) Complex inter-Grids are being built, tested, and deployed in the R&D domain. These are signs that the Grid momentum is still building, and the market is moving forward. The key to successfully penetrate the market will be to establish early deployments, so that the technology can evolve in parallel with the market requirements.

Grid Layers

At the base of the Grid architecture (the bottom layer so to speak) is the network, which assures the connectivity for the resources in the Grid (see Figure 1-1) [6]. On top of the network layer is the resource layer, which incorporates the actual resources that are part of the Grid (mainly computer and storage systems). The middle-ware layer (positioned above the resource layer) provides the tools that enable the various elements (servers, storage, and networks) to participate in a unified Grid environment. The middle-ware layer can be described as the intelligence that brings the various elements in the Grid together. The top layer of the Grid structure represents the application layer, which includes all different user applications (science, engineering, business, financial), as well as portals and development toolkits that are supporting the Grid applications. It is the top layer that the users of the Grid infrastructure are actually working with.

In most Grid architectures, the application layer also provides the *service-ware* functionality. The service-ware represents a set of general Grid management functions that are utilized to measure the amount of time a user spends on the Grid. Further, the service-ware acts as the billing functionality for the Grid services (assuming a commercial model), and keeps track of who is providing the resources and who can use them. It has to be pointed out that the service-ware is part of the top layer, as it is an entity the user interacts with, whereas the middle-ware components reflect a hidden layer that the user dose not necessarily has to worry about. There are other ways to describe this layered Grid structure. To illustrate, the Grid community uses the term *fabric* for all the physical infrastructure of the Grid, including the computers and the communication network. Within the middle-ware layer, distinctions can be made between a layer of resource and connectivity protocols, and a higher layer of collective services.

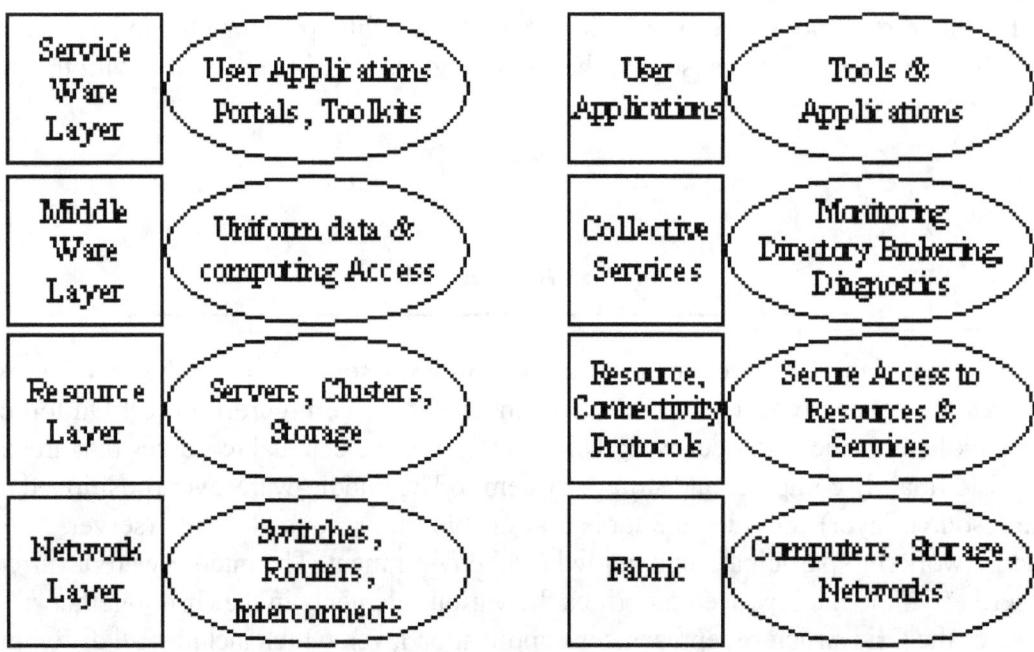

Figure 1-1: GRID Structures

Resource and connectivity protocols handle all the Grid specific network transactions (among different computers and any other resources on the Grid). This is accomplished via communication protocols, which let the resources communicate with each other, enabling the exchange of data, as well as authentication protocols, which provide secure mechanisms for verifying the identity of both users and resources. The collective services are also based on protocols (actual information protocols), which obtain information about the structure and state of the resources on the Grid, and management protocols that negotiate access to resources in a uniform way. These services include:

- Updating the directories that represent the available resources

- Providing brokering services (buy and sell resources)

- Monitoring the Grid and diagnosing any potential issues

- Replicating key data so that multiple copies are available at different locations for ease of use

- Providing membership/policy services, keeping track of who is allowed to do what and when

To reiterate, in all the Grid schemes, the top layer represents the applications layer. Applications rely on all the other layers to run on the Grid. To illustrate, assuming a Grid application that analyzes data that is distributed among several independent files. Hence, the application has to:

1. Obtain the necessary authentication credentials to open the files (resource and connectivity protocols)

2. Query an information system and replica catalogue to determine where the copies of the files can be located on the Grid, as well as where the computational resources necessary to conduct the analysis are available, and most conveniently located (collective services)

3. Submit actual requests to the fabric, the appropriate computers, storage systems, and network components to extract the data, initiate computations, and provide the results (resource and connectivity protocols)

4. Monitor the progress of the various computation tasks and data transfer components. Notifying the user when the analysis is completed. Detecting and responding to any potential failure conditions (collective services)

In order to accomplish all the above discussed scenarios, an application written for a single CPU system will have to be *substantially adapted* in order to invoke the proper services, use multiple distributed components simultaneously, and utilize the required protocols. In other words, a Grid requires companies and institutions to heavily invest time and money into getting their applications ready for a Grid environment [2]. Further, it has to be pointed out that not every application is suitable for running on a Grid.

Grid Applications

It is paramount to clearly define the type of applications that have the potential to run in a Grid environment, so that the right Grid project can be chosen, realistic expectations can be set, and performance, reliability, availability, maintainability, and scalability goals can be established and met. Typically, applications that are good candidates for a Grid implementation take many hours (possibly days or weeks) to execute and hence work on a large problem size. In some circumstances, the task is so big that it can not be completed at all even given today's processor capacity. The reason behind the long run time may be due to the application requiring many replicated runs of the same fundamental tasks, such as identical processing on many subgroups of a large data file, or certain types of optimizations or statistical simulations [3]. Another example of a long-running task may be the one where many independent tasks have to execute against the same large data source (scoring or risk analysis projects). In general, an application should possess one or more of the following characteristics to be considered a good candidate for a Grid implementation.

1. Problem to be solved results in a long execution time

2. Problem to be solved involves many replicated runs of the same fundamental task

3. Problem to be solved requires processing vast amounts of data

4. Problem to be solved allows the decomposition into multiple execution or data sets

Many (especially scientific) applications involve repeating the same fundamental task many times against unique subsets of the data pool. While the execution of a single task against a single subset of the data may execute rather quickly, repeating the same task against thousands or even millions of subsets of the data pool impacts the aggregate execution time. These types of problems are massively parallel and the applications that solve them are very well suited to a Grid implementation, as the replicated tasks can be distributed across the Grid and executed in parallel, which greatly reduces the aggregate execution time. Each of the fundamental tasks distributed across the Grid has to have access to all the required (input) data. Sometimes the input data can be small (MB's), and other times the input data may be rather large (GB's). In order to achieve the highest possible efficiency level, the compute nodes have to spend the majority of the time processing compute tasks rather than processing any communication related activities. Compute tasks that require substantial data movement generally do not perform very well in a Grid environment. The data has to be either distributed to the nodes prior to running the application, or the data has to be made available via a shared network storage solution. It has to be pointed out though that there have been many recent advances in data storage hardware (switches, controllers, disks) and software (advanced parallel file systems for clusters) that provide faster access to data, and hence actively contribute to the success of a Grid implementation.

Globus Grid Toolkit

Practically all major (R&D) Grid projects today are built based on protocols and services provided by the Globus Toolkit, a software solution which is being developed by the Globus Alliance. This research effort involves primarily Ian Foster's team at Argonne National Laboratory and Carl Kesselman's team at the University of Southern California in Los Angeles [9]. The toolkit provides a set of software tools to implement the basic services and capabilities required to construct a computational Grid (such as security, resource location, resource management, and communications). Below is a list of the primary elements included in the Globus Toolkit.

- *Globus Resource Allocation Manager (GRAM)*. The GRAM processes the resource requests, and allocates the resources necessary for application execution. The component further manages active jobs that are running on a Grid, and returns updated capability information to the Monitoring and Discovery Service (MDS).

- *Monitoring and Discovery Service (MDS)*. A Light-way Directory Access Protocol (LDAP) based service that allows querying system information from a variety of components (processing capacity, bandwidth capacity, types of storage) [8]. MDS enables the collection of element specific information for use in a Grid environment. It allows the optional construction of a uniform namespace (for resource information purposes) across a system that may involve many organizations.

- *Grid Security Infrastructure (GSI)*. Provides a secure authentication and communication facility over a Grid network. In addition, it supports security across organizational boundaries, and single sign-on capabilities for the users of a Grid, including delegation of credentials for computations that involve multiple resources. GSI is based on public key encryption (X.509 certificates), and secure sockets layer (SSL) entities, with extensions for Grid-specific applications.

- *Grid Resource Information Service (GRIS)*. Provides a uniform approach to querying resources on a Grid for their current configuration, capabilities, and status information, respectively. Such resources may include server systems, storage and network components, or database systems.

- *Grid Index Information Service (GIIS)*. Provides a method to coordinate arbitrary GRIS services to provide a consistent system image, which can be explored by Grid enabled applications. In addition to providing a consistent system image, subsets of GRIS services (such as all the storage entities within a specific subset of a Grid) can be defined.

- *GridFTP*. A high-performance, secure, and robust data transfer mechanism for Grid environments. GridFTP is based on FTP (the File Transfer Protocol), but is provided with extensions for Grid-specific requirements. Additional features include third-party control over data transfer, parallel data transfer, striped data transfer, and partial file transfer.

- *Replica Catalog*. Provides a mechanism for maintaining a catalog of data-set replicas. This service is accomplished by providing actual mapping information among logical file names and one or more copies of the files location on physical storage.

- *Replica Management*. Provides a mechanism that couples the Replica Catalog and the GridFTP technologies, allowing applications to generate and manage replicas of large data-set entities.

To reiterate, many of the functions performed by the Grid middle-ware and/or the Grid server appliances today (including security, quality of service, fault detection and recovery, policy management, scheduling and queuing, authentication, topology discovery, resource allocation, and load balancing) are natural tasks for today's networking products and protocols [5]. Hence, many of the protocols and functions defined by the Globus Toolkit are analogous to protocols that already exist in the networking and storage environment, but the toolkit provides the services optimized for Grid-specific deployments. The synergy between Grid protocols defined at the middle-ware layer and protocols at other layers (networking and storage), are expected to pragmatically converge over time. Applications enabled for Grid computing represent an actual convergence point for storage, networking, and computing resources, respectively. There are two main reasons for the strength and popularity of the Globus toolkit. (1) The Grid will have to support a wide variety of applications that have been developed according to different programming paradigms. Rather than providing a uniform programming model for Grid applications, the Globus Toolkit reflects an object-oriented approach, providing a set of services from which developers can choose based on a company's particular needs. The tools can be introduced one at a time (into existing programs) to allow the application to gradually become increasingly Grid enabled. To illustrate, an application may exploit some of the Globus features such as GRAM for resource management or GRIS for information services, without necessarily utilizing the Globus security or replica management systems, respectively. (2) Similar to the Linux operating system, the providers of the Globus Toolkit are distributing the software under the open-source licensing agreement. This allows other institutions and single contributors to utilize the software at no cost, as well as to contribute via improvements to the toolkit.

Summary - Benefits of Grid computing

There are several economic and business factors that are contributing to the heightened interest in the development and deployment of Grid computing. Based on the Internet and E-commerce, today's society is inundated with data. As the available data repository grows bigger and wider, the window of opportunity for capturing and translating the available data into information shrinks rapidly. Computing applications in many industries involve processing vast amounts of data and/or performing large numbers of repetitive computation operations that exceed the capabilities of existing platforms. To utilize data analysis techniques to achieve a high level of business intelligence, and improve the decision making process, data has to be analyzed in a much more timely manner. Today's business requirements demand a much larger sample size for analysis to provide the best possible accuracy level achievable. The challenges that IT faces today include budget cuts, server consolidation, hardware provisioning and overall administration, all factors that may further drive the interest in implementing Grid computing. The convergence of recent hardware and software advances has made resource virtualization feasible, hence made it easier to construct and deploy a Grid infrastructure. On the hardware side, advances include networked storage devices and low-cost, modular hardware components (such as blade systems). On the software side, the advances include improvements in networking, Web services, databases, application servers and management frameworks. While Grid computing may not be the solution for every application or institution, Grid computing has to be considered as an innovative solution that provides:

1. Scalability of applications, as long-running applications can be decomposed along either execution unit boundaries and/or data subsets, and hence be executed in parallel, economizing on the aggregate execution time.

2. Scalability in the number of users, as multiple users can access a virtualized pool of resources to obtain the best possible response time by maximizing the utilization of the computing resources.

3. By implementing Grid computing technology, organizations can optimize the return on investment and lower the cost of ownership

Therefore, Grid solutions reflect three main categories beneficial to organizations and institutions. (1) Cost saving, as it is feasible to leverage and exploit unutilized or underutilized compute power and/or storage capacity within a networked environment. (2) Improved business agility by decreasing the time to process the data and deliver the results. By delivering results faster, a company is provided with the insight and agility to adjust to a changing market place. (3) Enhanced collaboration as IT resources can be shared and utilized collectively. This collaboration insures to efficiently, as well as effectively resolve compute-intensive problems.

References

1.   Avery, P., Foster, I., Gardner, R., Newman, H. and Szalay, A." An International Virtual-Data Grid Laboratory for Data Intensive Science". GriPhyN, 2001

2.   Czajkowski, K., Fitzgerald, S., Foster, I. and Kesselman, C., "Grid Information Services for Distributed Resource Sharing". In IEEE International Symposium on High Performance Distributed Computing, (2001), IEEE Press

3.   Foster, I., "Grid Technologies & Applications: Architecture & Achievements", Argonne National Laboratory, 2002

4.   Foster, I. and Kesselman, C. "A Data Grid Reference Architecture". GriPhyN, 2001

5.   Foster, I. and Kesselman, C. "Globus: A Toolkit-Based Grid Architecture. In The Grid: Blueprint for a New Computing Infrastructure", Morgan Kaufmann, 1999, 259-278.

6.   Grid @ CERN: http://gridcafe.web.cern.ch/gridcafe/GridatCERN/gridatcern.html

7.   Oracle, "Oracle Grid Computing", Oracle Business While Paper, 2003

8.   Smith, W., Gunter, D., "Simple LDAP Schemas for Grid Monitoring", NASA Ames Research Center, 2001

9.   The Globus Alliance: http://www.globus.org/

Chapter 2 - Parallel Systems & File System Technologies in a Cluster Environment

Introduction

Local file systems support a persistent name space. A local file system views devices as being locally attached, the devices are not shared, and hence there is no need in the file system design to enforce device-sharing semantics. Instead, the focus is on aggressively caching and aggregating file system operations to improve performance by economizing on the number of actual disk accesses required for each file system operation. Newer networking technologies allow multiple machines (nodes) to share storage devices. IBM' General Parallel File System (GPFS) or Red Hat' Global File System are representing distributed file system technologies that are taking a shared, network-attached storage approach. These file systems are built on the premise that a shared disk file system has to exist within the context of a cluster infrastructure, and has to provide proper error handling and recovery (performance, availability, and scalability features are key requirements as well). In a storage area network (SAN) attached environment, SAN clients may only manage local file system requests and act as file managers for there own I/O operations. Hence, the storage devices (the IO subsystem) serve the data directly to the clients. A cluster file system design provides transparent parallel access to storage devices while maintaining standard UNIX file system semantics. User applications only view a single logical device via the standard open(), close(), read(), write() and fcntl() primitives. This transparency is paramount in regards to ease of use, as well as to the portability of these file system technologies. To reiterate, a cluster file system based design differs from traditional, local file systems, by emphasizing sharing, connectivity, as well as (client side) caching. Unlike local file systems such as IBM's J2 or SGI' XFS, contemporary cluster file systems distribute file system resources (including the metadata) across the entire storage subsystem, which allows simultaneous access from multiple machines.

The goal of this chapter is to elaborate on the terminology's surrounding parallel systems and the file systems that are being used in a cluster based environment. Some of the terms actually overlap, which may result in misconceptions and confusion on the user site, an issue that is addressed in this chapter. Further, this chapter discusses the classification of some the applications that may be executed on a cluster. To illustrate cluster file system technologies, the last part of this chapter introduces IBM's GPFS and Red Hat's GFS file system, focusing on architecture, setup, configuration, and availability options. Further, some of the performance related features embedded into the GPFS and GFS framework are discussed and elaborated.

Parallel Systems

The majority of today's parallel computing market is focused on small and medium scale Symmetric Multiprocessor (SMP) systems. Built with two to 64 processors, these SMP systems are designed with a global memory subsystem, hardware support for cache coherence, and are managed by a single kernel. SMP systems provide support for a *shared memory* based programming model. This model uses a global name space for data and assumes implicit communication and data caching. The use of the *shared memory* model reduces implementation complexity when developing applications that require parallel functions. A programmer is in control of the application's parallel activity by using simple control constructs that are available within the programming language statements. Thus, irregular data access and communication patterns are more efficiently controlled within the domain of the application. Because of the extensive use of SMP machines, the *shared memory* programming style has gained a great deal of exposure and therefore has reduced the learning curve for programmers and developers alike [15].

Contemporary large parallel systems support a distributed memory architecture paradigm. Data sharing in these systems is accomplished by using either a *message passing* or a *distributed shared memory* based programming model. These programming styles are significantly different from an SMP *shared memory* model; consequently organizations that are required to scale their applications beyond the levels supported by SMP systems are faced with a critical decision. They must either invest in the development of new applications, or restructure existing applications to utilize either a *message passing* or a *distributed shared memory* approach. Programming tools provide abstractions from the details of the physical architecture. The use of a language compiler can exploit the *distributed shared memory* model during the software development phase in a technical computing environment. For example, High Performance Fortran utilizes the shared memory subsystem that is present in the system architecture [20]. In most commercial computing systems, a middleware layer will provide the programming environment. The middleware layer incorporates the shared memory support in the same manner as that of a language compiler [14]. By using an interface definition language (IDL) in conjunction with a programming language, the developer builds the distributed application. As an additional feature, a middleware layer can incorporate the parallel paradigm by abstracting the application from any system details. This refinement can improve an application's performance without modifying the original code. Today, many large parallel systems support either the shared memory or the message passing programming model. Systems that support both are in the best competitive position for future technical and commercial computing markets. However, the communication support for any parallel architecture must be highly available and must scale.

Parallel Architectures

The parallel systems discussed in this chapter are in the class of machines known as Multiple Instruction Multiple Data Stream (MIMD). These systems are composed of multiple processors, each independently operating on their own data stream. Figure 2-1 depicts the decomposition of MIMD systems into three categories, Uniformed Memory Access (UMA), Distributed Shared Memory (DSM), and Message Passing (MPS) systems. The UMA design provides all CPU's with equal access to memory. The familiar SMP machines are an example of an UMA system. DSM and MPP systems are composed of local and remote memory subsystems. Therefore in DSM as well as MPP systems, some memory accesses are local to a processor while others are to remote blocks. These systems are categorized as either a *distributed shared memory* or a *message passing* system based on the node-to-node communication mechanism.

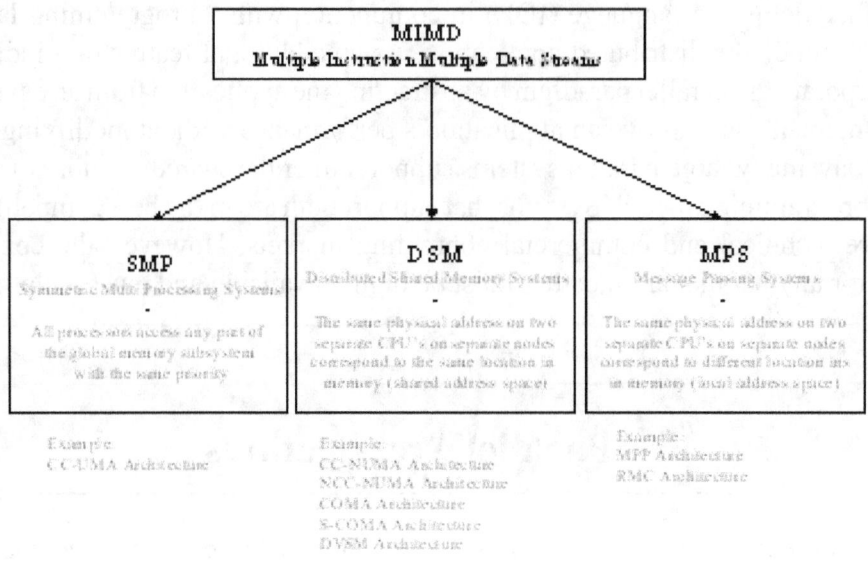

Figure 2-1: Parallel Architecture

Communication and Memory Architecture Models

Typical DSM and MPS systems use multiple memory subsystems that are physically distributed. On a DSM (sometimes in the literature referred to as Non Uniform Memory Access *NUMA* system) configuration, the separate memory subsystems can be addressed as one (logical) shared address space. Therefore the same physical address on two processors refers to the same location in memory. In a DSM system a processor can make a reference to any authorized memory location [19], thus data communication is achieved implicitly via load and store operations. Because of these machine-level instructions, data access in a DSM system is dependent upon the location of the data word in physical memory. In contrast to a shared address space, the design of an MPS parallel system consists of multiple, private address-spaces that are logically disjoint. In these systems, the same physical address on two different processors refers to a different location in each of the memory subsystems. Thus, each processor-memory module is essentially a separate computer [14]. In these systems, data communication is accomplished by explicitly passing messages among the processors (messages are used to either request an action or deliver data). For example, if a processor requires access to data in a remote memory subsystem, it will send a data request message to the remote node. In this scenario, the message can be considered as being a form of a remote procedure call (RPC).

In an RPC implementation, the destination processor receives a message and performs the requested operation on behalf of the remote processor. The circle is completed when the outcome of the request is returned to the source via a reply message. Traditional RPC communication is synchronous, since the initiating processor sends a request and waits until the reply is returned before resuming activity [8]. The implementation of a subsystem that supports request-reply communication requires a good deal of complexity. Most RPC implementations are designed to encapsulate the details of sending and receiving messages, including passing complex arguments. Applications that require request-reply communication can be implemented with an RPC facility, thus abstracting the developer from the underlying details. Other communication libraries being used in an MPS cluster environment provide an asynchronous communication mechanism and are based on Active Messages [22]. An Active Message includes the address of a user-specified handler. When the Active Message arrives at the target process, the specified handler is invoked and executes in the address space of that process. An Active Message operation can be considered as being unilateral in the sense that the target process does not have to take any explicit action for the Active Message to complete.

Parallel Application Performance

Algorithmic constraints may play a decisive role in determining the amount of parallelism possible for any given application. From a software perspective, parallelism within a program may occur at many different levels. A c*oarse-grain* design indicates that the units of parallelism are of a significant length of duration relative to the whole program and usually refers to parallelism implemented at a very high level of a program. In a *fine-grain* design the units of parallelism are of relatively short duration and usually describe loop-level parallelization or data parallelism. As noted by Koenigs [16], performance of a real-world application running on a parallel system is a difficult quantity to measure. Some scientific applications model a complex interplay of phenomena, which may involve the coupling of different time scales and packages (physics and chemistry) into a dynamic framework. In contrast, commercial Relational Database Management Systems (RDBMS) deal with large working sets and complex code as well as a shared data set, which contributes to a data partition problem. The underling issue for any application is the period of time that is required to solve a given problem. Raw CPU time cannot be considered as the main performance indicator, as the CPU time dos not account for communication overhead. Another factor to consider is that throughput optimization may result in performing some operations multiple times to avoid the overhead associated with broadcasting the results to too many processors. In other cases, it is desirable to perform multiple sets of instructions on a single set of data and to retain only one set of results. Both cases inflate the overhead of computing a result, but do so in the fastest possible manner.

Programming Models and Methods

For SMP as well as DSM systems, most programming models include either a *work sharing* or a *data parallel* based approach. In a *work sharing* paradigm, a single thread executes until it encounters a parallel construct (such as a parallel loop), at which point the work is divided among a group of threads. After all the threads complete the *processing part of the parallel construct*, control returns to a single thread. In a *data parallel* approach the parallel constructs are implicit in the array syntax used for specially designed objects. In both models, the location of the data may determine where the execution of the instruction referencing the data item will actually occur [15].

In the case of an MPS system, models designed to work across multiple address spaces are based on *message* and *data passing* libraries. In these models, the threads operate in relative independence and explicitly communicate through function calls to the communication library. Examples of *message passing* models include the Message Passing Interface (MPI) or the Parallel Virtual Machine (PVM) implementation. Examples of data-passing models include the SHMEM library from SGI or the Bulk Synchronous Parallel library form the University of Oxford [16]. DSM systems map individual processor's memory into a single shared memory space. Each task running in a DSM system has equal access to memory, thus the programming models have to incorporate a synchronization mechanism to preserve data integrity. The DSM mechanism abstracts the application from the details of the interprocess communication and promotes application portability. Programming in DSM systems consist of object registration, exclusive object access, object modification, and the propagation of the modified object [24]. An example of the DSM effort is OpenMP which provides support for multiple languages (FORTRAN, C & C++) and architectures (different versions of the UNIX & Windows operating system). Other ongoing work exists in the area of Java DSM [24], as well as in a new operating system that integrates the DSM capability (called RHODOS) [23]. Parallelism can either be achieved by utilizing a pipeline or a partitioning based approach. In the case of a pipeline, processed data is moved to the next *stage* as the resource becomes available. Partitioning involves dividing the data into separate sections, processing the individual sections in parallel, and finally combing the output stream [15]. An application that consists of sequential algorithms is evaluated by the correctness of its output. With parallel applications, the objective is not only to produce the correct output, but to either decrease the execution time by adding more CPU's or to process a larger data set by utilizing additional resources.

Performance Metrics for Communication Mechanisms

In parallel systems, inter-node communication is the pipeline that facilitates remote processing. Performance of this communication channel is vital to the overall systems throughput. In order to understand the issues involved in inter-node performance, the following categories outline the concerns any MIMD communication mechanism has to address:

1. *Communication Bandwidth*. Preferably, the communication bandwidth is limited by processor, memory, and interconnection bandwidth rather than by some aspect of the communication mechanism itself. During communication, node resources involved in the communication process are occupied, preventing other outbound or inbound communication. If this occurs for each and every message, the ramification is that there is an absolute limit that is being set for the communication bandwidth.

2. *Communication Latency*. Ideally the latency should be as low as possible. The communication mechanism and its implementation largely determine the software and the hardware overhead when sending and receiving messages. The latency is crucial as it affects performance as well as the program design that is used in a multiprocessor environment. Unless the latency is hidden, it directly affects performance either by tying up processor resources or by causing the processor to be in a *wait state*.

3. *Communication Latency Hiding.* The main question is if the communication mechanism can hide the latency. This can be accomplished by overlapping communication with either local computation or another form of communication. Although measuring this point is not as simple as measuring communication bandwidth or latency, it is an important characterization. Latency hiding can be quantified by measuring the run-time on machines that have the same communication latency, but incorporate different support structures.

As discussed by Schoinas [21], each of these performance measurements is influenced by the characteristics of the communication mechanisms required by the application. The size of the data items is the most obvious, since it directly affects both latency and bandwidth. Further, the size affects the efficiency of different latency hiding techniques. Similarly, the regularity in the communication patterns affect the cost of naming and protection, and hence the communication overhead. Consequently, mechanisms that perform well on variable-sized data communication requests, as well as on regular and irregular communication patterns, support a larger spectrum of applications.

Shared Memory Architectures

Shared memory programming models may be supported by a variety of physical architectures. Some of the architectures discussed in this chapter can be considered as actual research projects. Nevertheless, it is paramount for the reader to have a certain degree of understanding of the terminology used in a parallel environment, such as:

*   Cache Coherent Uniform Memory Access (CC-UMA)

*   Massively Parallel Processing (MPP)

*   Replicated Memory Cluster (RMC)

*   Cache Coherent Non Uniform Memory Access (CC-NUMA)

*   Non Cache Coherent Non Uniform Memory Access (NCC-NUMA)

*   Cache Only Memory Access (COMA)

*   Distributed Virtual Shared Memory (DVSM)

    *   Simple Cache Only Memory Access (S-COMA)

Cache Coherent Uniform Memory Access Architecture

The Cache Coherent Uniform Memory Access (CC-UMA) architecture is the most prevalent approach in terms of shared memory parallel computer systems. In this design, all processors can access any part of the global physical memory subsystem with the same performance. The system is controlled by one operating system kernel and features a shared I/O space. CC-UMA systems provide a convenient model for parallelism. The actual communication is accomplished via shared memory, which implies that the memory location of the data objects is not an issue. Smaller CC-UMA systems use a shared memory bus utilizing a snooping logic that is built into the cache controllers [14]. Each cache controller *listens* to all the memory access requests on the bus and intervenes if a cache coherence action is required. Larger systems use a memory switch and require multiple directory structures to maintain cache coherence. The directories keep track of the location of each cached line and are used to identify the cache controllers that must be active to satisfy a request to load or store a cache line [15]. A cache controller is involved in a request if its cache contains an exclusive copy of a line that another processor attempts to access or update.

Unfortunately, CC-UMA architectures do not scale very well. A shared memory bus cannot effectively support the memory bandwidth requirements of more than a few modern microprocessors. As the requirement of the number of CPU's and memory ports increase, the cost of a memory switch becomes prohibitive. Further, the latency of the global memory and the performance of the cache coherence protocols degrade as a result of the increased CPU numbers. The system software for larger CC-UMA systems is adversely affected. The task of scaling an operating system kernel to a level where is efficient and effective to manage 32 or more processors is a daunting task [25]. Kernel scalability faces an inherent constraint, in that a logically centralized system would be further taxed with the service of an increased number of system events. More importantly, there is the practical obstacle of significantly restructuring a kernel that has evolved over many years and was modified by hundreds of developers.

Another disadvantage of traditional CC-UMA systems can be found in the area of fault tolerance. The outage of any processor or memory card might result into a global system failure. The probability of a failure is proportional to the number of CPU's, thus reducing the reliability of a larger system. Such an outage can be prevented on newer systems that support hot-swappable CPU's and dynamic resource re-allocation among logical partitions in an SMP environment. CC-UMA configurations with 2 to 16 processors are commonly being used, and systems with 32 to 64 CPU's are available from some of the major hardware vendors. The high-end server configurations are implemented by compromising the performance of each processor by offering reduced per processor memory bandwidth. While the practical size of CC-UMA systems is expected to slowly increase, there is little likelihood that CC-UMA systems with hundreds of processors will be practical in the near future.

Massively Parallel Processing Architecture

Massively Parallel Processing (MPP) systems traditionally consist of one or more CPU's per node, a local memory subsystem, local I/O, and one instance of the Operating System (OS) per node. A custom interconnect provides the communication facility among the nodes. The connection among the nodes does not require any hardware coherency, because each node has its own copy of the OS and therefore its own unique physical memory address space. Coherency is implemented in software via a message-passing mechanism. Messaged-based software coherency latency is typically hundreds of times slower than hardware coherency latency, but less expensive to implement [8].

MPP systems sacrifice latency in order to achieve connectivity, which allows the potential connection of hundreds of nodes (high scalability). The overall performance of an MPP system is notoriously sensitive to the latency of the software-based message passing protocol, which is impacted by the underlying hardware medium. In general, (application) performance tuning on MPP systems involves partitioning the data to minimize the amount of information that has to be passed among the nodes. Applications that have a natural partitioning in the data stream (such as video on demand) run efficiently on MPP systems [9]. The majority of the inter-node traffic on an MPP system is shared data. The sharing of data between processors inside an SMP node requires no data movement since all processors access the same shared memory subsystem. When data has to be shared among multiple memory subsystems, the data has to be either replicated or transferred from one memory subsystem to another. Repeated processor access to data residing in memory of a remote node imposes unacceptable time delays [18]. Based on this scenario, data sharing among nodes is rather slow and very complex. Access delays explain why MPP performance is best suited for applications that operate in a statically partitioned processing environment.

Replicated Memory Cluster Architecture

A Replicated Memory Cluster (RMC) consists of two or more nodes where:

* Each node is running its own copy of the OS

* Each node is running its own copy of the parallel application

* The nodes share a common pool of resources (such as disk drives)

In a classic MPP system, nodes do not share the storage resources. The sharing of storage resources is the primary difference between a clustered SMP system and a traditional MPP configuration. In a cluster, separate instances of the application have to be aware of each other. Each instance must execute a locking mechanism to maintain coherency within the application before attempting to update any part of the common storage pool [25]. Locking makes a cluster more difficult to manage and scale as compared to a single SMP node. However, a cluster offers several advantages such as continuous application availability in the case of a single node failure, as well as superior overall performance. The emergence of parallel file systems for MPP and RMC systems contributes significantly to the scalability of the I/O subsystem, as well as to a much improved application throughput performance in a cluster environment.

Cache Coherent Non Uniform Memory Access Architecture

The Cache Coherent Non Uniform Memory Access (CC-NUMA) architecture alleviates some of the issues that can be found in the CC-UMA design by providing non-uniform access to the memory subsystems. The physical address space is distributed among all nodes in the system and is managed by a single, global Virtual Memory Manager (VMM). Each processor can access its local memory with high bandwidth and low latency [6], while access to remote memory subsystems is provided at a lower performance. This reduces the cost of supporting global memory access. The system is still managed by one operating system kernel, and provides the same logical architecture as a CC-UMA system. Data caching is accomplished in regular hardware caches. A CC-NUMA system can be built from standard single-processor or SMP nodes.

A shared memory adapter is attached to the shared memory bus and controls the communication with other nodes. This adapter handles all memory requests that access physical memory on this node, whether the requests originated on the local or a remote node. The adapter further handles requests to invalidate a line in a local cache on behalf of the remote nodes. The memory controller participates in requests that originate on the local node and require access to a real memory subsystem on a remote node. The adapter has to maintain directory information for lines in the local memory subsystem that are cached in remote nodes [7]. The information is required to satisfy load and store instructions to the local memory subsystem (in the case where remote cache controllers must be involved in the memory access). The IEEE Scaleable Coherent Interface (SCI) provides a standard for these memory adapters.

A CC-NUMA design performs well in the case where the majority of processor memory accesses are to the local memory subsystem. Since processors have no immediate control over memory allocation in a virtual memory system, locality has to be provided by the VMM working in conjunction with the scheduler and the dispatcher. The scheduler provides affinity scheduling to ensure that a thread is preferentially scheduled on the same processor throughout its lifetime. The VMM may copy frequently accessed read-only pages to the nodes where they are most frequently being used. Interfaces may be provided to the user or compiler to control or influence the data location [7]. These mechanisms will not enhance locality of access to shared pages. If a shared page is equally accessed by two processors on two different nodes at a granularity that is too fine for the page migration mechanism to be effective, then at least one processor will access the pages remotely. In any case, the reaction time of a page migration scheme is likely to be too slow for many irregular parallel codes. Scalability and fault tolerance still present major design and implementation issues that will have to be further addressed. Examples of CC-NUMA systems include the Stanford University Flash and the MIT Alewife systems.

Non Cache Coherent Non Uniform Memory Access Architecture

The Non Cache Coherent, Non Uniform Memory Access (NCC-NUMA) architecture is essentially similar to a CC-NUMA implementation (without incorporating the mechanisms to keep global data coherent). In a NCC-NUMA system, it is the responsibility of software components (either the application or the compiler) to manage the use of data objects so that *stale data* is not inadvertently seen by the application [11]. A NCC-NUMA system is easier to build than a CC-NUMA system as complex coherence mechanisms are not required. Further, NCC-NUMA systems have a potential for higher performance, as it is possible for intelligent software components to either avoid or anticipate cache coherence actions.

NCC-NUMA operations are incompatible with SMP systems, and place considerably more emphasis on software components when it comes to data management. As an example, if a node has finished updating a data object and would like to make it available to other nodes, a software component has to issue an instruction sequence to flush the data back to the global memory subsystem. At the same time, software configured on the other nodes has to explicitly discard any copies of the data object that they are caching to ensure that future references will only fetch the updated copy of the data object. The Cray T3D and T3E are examples of NCC-NUMA systems in use.

Cache Only Memory Access Architecture

A Cache Only Memory Access (COMA) based architecture increases the amount of local cache per node, extending the memory hierarchy by one level and so reducing the chances of an actual remote memory access. Many large-scale parallel applications exhibit algorithmic locality. By utilizing larger caches, the frequency of global inter-node communication is reduced. Hardware Level 1 (L1) and Level 2 (L2) caches are normally built from expensive, high speed Static Random Access Memory (SRAM) components. In order to provide a larger cache at a reasonable cost, it is necessary to take advantage of less expensive and slower Dynamic Random Access Memory (DRAM) components. Main memory is composed of DRAM chips. By using a portion of main memory as an additional cache, a third caching level, Level 3 (L3) is generated in the memory hierarchy.

This is the basic idea that is pursued by COMA systems. In conjunction with a cache controller and an SRAM cache directory, the entire physical memory subsystem is utilized as an additional cache [12] [17]. This study showed that the COMA architecture suffers from several serious drawbacks. In COMA, the structure of the memory subsystem is quite different from a conventional memory subsystem. The ramification is that because the standard memory controllers cannot be used in COMA, additional hardware controllers have to be developed to mange the L3 cache. Further, significant changes are required in the memory management software to support the new paradigm. Finally, the issues of kernel scalability and fault tolerance will have to be revisited. Examples of COMA systems in use today include the Kendall Square Research KSR-1 or the Swedish Institute of Computer Science (SICS) Data Diffusion Machine.

Distributed Virtual Shared Memory Architecture

The Distributed Virtual Shared Memory (DVSM) architecture provides a shared memory interface on a distributed memory system that does not require any additional hardware support. The DVSM technology leverages the standard hardware support for page protection (where page sized cache lines are being used). The status of the cache lines is maintained by utilizing the protection information in the page frame table. An access to an invalid page will cause a page fault. In this scenario, the VMM will invoke an external pager that executes the cache coherence protocol in software, possibly copying data from a remote node to the local memory subsystem. As a result, the state of the pages will be updated ad hoc [10]. This study showed that this scheme has potential. DVSM is being executed on top of a distributed memory system, where each node is controlled by a separate OS kernel. This enhances availability and reliability; the loss of a single node will not effect the system as a whole. No additional (expensive) hardware is required, thus reducing the complexity and cost of the system. No changes have to be made to the structure of the operating system, because most contemporary systems support external pagers as kernel extensions. The local memory at each node is used as a cache, allowing for very large, inexpensive L3 caches. DVSM nicely addresses the scalability issues found in other architectures, as management of the global virtual shared memory subsystem is separated from virtual memory management. Likewise, extensions for fault tolerance only affect a separate DVSM layer. This author believes that despite some of the positive facts outlined here, the major issue with a DVSM based approach can be found in the area of performance. Satisfying a page fault in software is much slower (a few orders of a magnitude) than satisfying a cache miss in hardware [14]. The execution of the page fault software handler disrupts pipelines and caches in the processor, and the large size of the cache lines proposed for DVSM systems causes significant false sharing overhead. Although a lot of research has been conducted to improve the performance of DVSM systems, the argument made is that it is unlikely that such a pure software based solution will result into a competitive large-scale shared memory production system. Examples of DVSM systems include the Princeton IVY and the Intel Paragon systems.

Simple Cache Only Memory Access Architecture

Simple Cache Only Memory Access (S-COMA) has been proposed in the literature as a way to consolidate the advantages of DVSM and COMA systems. As discussed by Liberty [17], such systems can be built from standard single-processor or SMP nodes. Functionally, an S-COMA system allows a programmer to view shared data in the same way as other shared memory architectures. S-COMA is a system organization that ties together a distributed system in a way that allows a parallel or distributed application to share data implicitly, via normal load and store instructions. Programs can attach shared memory areas the same way as with the UNIX System V shared memory implementation. Similar to COMA based systems, S-COMA extends the memory hierarchy by one more level, utilizing a portion of the large and inexpensive DRAM memory subsystem as an additional cache. Data is either migrated or replicated at each of these new cache subsystems on a ad-hoc basis to fulfill the demands of memory references [12]. However, rather than modifying the node memory controller to manage the cache (such as in COMA), cache management becomes a function of simplified software and hardware components. The S-COMA architecture introduces an additional hardware adapter that attaches to the nodes shared memory interconnect. It traps global memory references and initiates protocol processing. The design of such an adapter is similar to the one that is being used in a CC-NUMA system [13]. The only exception is that an access to remote memory cannot be identified by the physical address, as this address has to be extracted out of the local page frame table that caches the remote page. Instead, the adapter needs to maintain a directory with entries for each local page frame that caches a remote page.

The adapter snoops on the bus and intervenes when it recognizes this type of access. As with DVSM systems, system software that is being invoked during a page fault supports the management of the global memory subsystem. From an application perspective, S-COMA allows programs to share data in the same way as on an SMP system. Shared memory segments are attached by different instances of the program, and the data in the segments is referenced by regular load and store instructions. The application does not have to determine on which node the shared data resides. From a systems perspective, S-COMA retains the advantages of multiple operating system instances. Each node is autonomous providing greater flexibility, as well as higher availability and scalability. When an application that operates on different nodes specifies a memory segment that has to be shared, the global shared memory subsystem is responsible for managing the data among all the nodes that participate in the transaction.

The S-COMA approach has the advantage of providing hardware support for cache coherence, allowing shared memory access at the same speed as on a CC-NUMA system. At the same time, S-COMA allows the use of local DRAM memory as a large L3 cache and does not require a global virtual memory manager layer. Instead, it has a software structure that is very similar to the one that can be found in a DVSM system [17]. Further, the access speed to private memory is not reduced (as it is the case in a COMA environment). S-COMA introduces another level to the memory hierarchy by utilizing a portion of the main memory subsystem of each node as an additional cache. Data in main memory is kept coherent with data in the node's L1 and L2 caches (via the node's existing cache coherence scheme). The cache coherence protocol within each of the nodes is extended by the S-COMA subsystem to other participating nodes. Globalization of memory addresses is accomplished by coordinating the separate nodes virtual memory managers and memory subsystems. Rather than performing extensive changes to the Virtual Memory Manager (as in NUMA), or applying complex changes to the node memory controller hardware itself (as in COMA), S-COMA utilizes a small extension to the VMM subsystem and an additional hardware adapter that connects to the system bus. In NUMA, the system's physical address space is distributed and shared at any time by all nodes in the cluster. A particular node may be called upon to provide the data from a particular address, even though that node may not be participating in the program execution [15] [17]. In S-COMA, sharing is performed at a virtual level. This is accomplished by having the parallel or distributed program attach only those portions of the data space that it has to share. The result is that the node participates in requesting and providing shared data only when the node is involved with the program that actually shares the data object.

Cluster File Systems and Cluster Applications

In general, cluster file systems complement the actual hardware and software cluster facilities in various ways. Traditionally, a cluster represents a group of nodes, acting as a single system. That definition may get stretched considerably though, as cluster technology today represents a dynamic field, encompassing a divers application spectrum that is continually absorbing new features [5]. Furthermore, cluster file system technologies, whether open source or proprietary, are rapidly converging in their capabilities. Many people in the industry refer to cluster applications and the underlying file system software being used as a *unit*. More accurately though, most clusters consist of two main components, (1) the nodes, which are connected to some sort of interconnect, and (2) the cluster file system, which acts as the software layer that enables the cluster nodes to share data and work together *as a unit*. In general, cluster applications can be classified based on their varying levels of maturity and capabilities:

- High performance clusters, which are also referred to as computational cluster systems. These systems are normally utilized to support very large data volumes (of computational processing). In such an environment, a parallel file system distributes the processing resources across the nodes, thereby allowing each node to access the same set of files concurrently (via concurrent read() and write() requests).

- High availability (HA) clusters, which are designed for fault tolerance or redundancy purposes. As these clusters normally use one or more servers (for data processing), the servers in the cluster are able to assume processing responsibilities in case that one or more of them goes down.

- Load balancing clusters distribute the workload as evenly as possible across multiple server systems, such as web or application servers, respectively.

- Storage cluster systems, which are utilized between Storage Area Network (SAN) components and server systems with different operating systems. These systems provide shared access to data blocks on a common storage media.

- Database cluster systems, such as Oracle's Real Application Cluster (RAC) platform, which introduce many of the cluster file system features into the application-layer itself.

Cluster File System Terminology

Cluster applications, such as the once mentioned above, provide overlapping features, and hence features of one or more of them are commonly found in a single cluster application (especially in a HA or load-balancing cluster environment) [3]. To illustrate, an Oracle RAC solution can be installed and configured over a HA cluster file system (to provide the benefits of database clustering to an actual HA cluster application). The filed of clustered file systems itself can be described as following:

- The term distributed file system reflects the generic description of a client-server or network file system, respectively. In such a scenario, the user data is not locally attached to a host system. In this category, NFS and CIFS are the most common distributed file systems being used today. It has to be pointed out that in NFS, there is a N:1 relationship between the nodes and the server system. Hence, in a general NFS environment, the NFS server represents a single point of failure.

- The term global file system refers to the actual namespace, in that all the files in the environment have the same name and path when viewed from all the nodes. Therefore, a global file system allows for a simple way to share data across nodes and users that are part of different entities of an organization. To illustrate, the WWW represents a global namespace, as a unique URL works from anywhere on this planet. AFS represents an early provider of a global namespace (/afs/cell-name), as it is feasible to assemble AFS cells from different organizations or institutions into a single shared file system.

- The term SAN file system represents a way to provide nodes with the capability to share Fibre Channel (FC) storage, a storage solution that is traditionally decomposed into private chunks that are bound to different hosts. To provide data sharing, a block-level metadata manager governs access to the different SAN devices. A SAN file system mounts storage natively on a node, but connects all the nodes to that storage, and distributes block addresses to the other nodes in the cluster. Some of the more popular SAN file systems in use today are SGI' cXFS, IBM' GPFS, or Red Hat' GFS.

- The term symmetric file system describes a file system in which the client nodes also have to run the metadata manager code. In other words, all the nodes in the cluster have an understanding of the underlying disk structure. An important point that has to be considered with a symmetric file system is the overhead (or lack therefor) that the metadata management places on the client nodes, serving both itself and other nodes. A non-efficient metadata implementation has a significant impact on the compute efficiency of the client nodes, and ultimately on the aggregate cluster performance. Some of the symmetric file systems in use today include Red Hat' GFS, IBM' GPFS, or HP' CFS.

- The term asymmetric file system reflects a file system solution where in the cluster, there are one or more dedicated metadata managers, which maintain the structural elements of the file system and its associated disk structure. Some of the asymmetric file systems in use include IBM' SanFS, Cluster File Systems' Lustre, or some of the more traditional file system solutions such as NFS and CIFS, respectively.

- The term cluster file system represents a distributed file system that does not have a single server with a set of clients (such as NFS), but instead consists of a cluster of server nodes that all collaborate to provide (high performance) service to the client base. To the client nodes in the cluster, this is all transparent, it is just a file system solution, but the file system software itself deals with distributing the requests to the elements that comprise the storage cluster. Some of the actual cluster file systems in use are HP' Tru64 cluster or Panasas' ActiveScale storage cluster file system.

- The term parallel file system describes a file system solution that supports parallel applications (such as MPI based scientific or life-science applications). In a parallel file system environment, all the nodes in the cluster may be accessing the same file (or files) at the same time, via concurrent read() and write() requests. Some parallel file systems in use today are IBM' GPFS, Cluster File Systems' Lustre, Panasas ActiveScale, or Red Hat' GFS.

It has to be pointed out that the terms discussed above overlap as well. To illustrate, a SAN file system may be symmetric or asymmetric, the environment may represent a parallel file system and/or a cluster file system based solution, respectively. As an example, Panasas' Storage Cluster and its ActiveScale File System represent a clustered, asymmetric, parallel, distributed file system solution. On the other hand, IBM's GPFS can be described as a parallel, symmetric file system solution that can be utilized in a SAN environment. There are of course many more file system solutions being used in a cluster environment today, but this article only focuses on some of the more popular once.

Introduction to IBM' General Parallel File System (GPFS)

The General Parallel File System (GPFS) represents IBM's parallel file system solution [2]. The actual file system is constructed from a collection of disks, which contain the file system data, a collection of nodes, which own and manage the file system, and a set of network connections (interconnects), which reflects the communication facility used among the nodes and the storage subsystem. In its simplest environment, the storage is connected to all the nodes by utilizing a SAN solution. Figure 2-1 represents a Fibre Channel (FC) SAN. The nodes are connected to the storage via the SAN, and to each other by utilizing a LAN solution. Data that is being used by the applications is transferred over the SAN, whereas the control information used among the GPFS instances on the cluster is transferred via the LAN component.

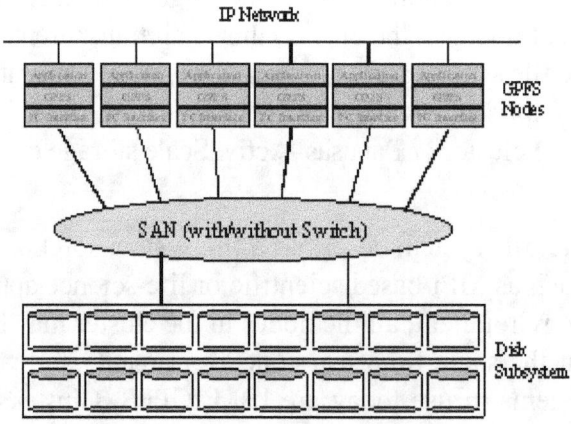

Figure 2-2: SAN Attached GPFS Cluster

In some cluster environments, where it is not feasible for every compute node to have direct access to the SAN, GPFS may be configured to utilize an (IBM provided) network block device capability. In an environment utilizing the IBM pSeries High Performance Switch (HPS), the capability is provided by the IBM Virtual Shared Disk (VSD) component, which is an AIX resource. In a Linux or AIX setup that utilizes any other interconnect infrastructure, GPFS uses the Network Shared Disk (NSD) capability, an actual component of GPFS. Both, VSD and NSD provide a software simulation of a SAN across either IP or an IBM proprietary network. GPFS uses NSD (and VSD if a HPS is present) to provide high-speed access to data for applications running on compute nodes that do not have a SAN attachment.

Data is served to those compute nodes from a VSD or an NSD I/O server, respectively. Multiple I/O servers for each disk are feasible (actually recommended) to avoid single point of failure situations. Figure 2-2 reflects a GPFS Linux setup. In such a configuration, data and control information are transferred across an un-switched LAN. Such a model is only appropriate for smaller GPFS clusters. Switched LAN environments and/or bonded LAN (such as bonded Gigabit Ethernet) setups are recommended for clusters that require significant data transfer rates. Naturally, higher performance interconnects such as the IBM HPS or InfiniBand provide even better performance (if the actual workload can be driven high enough to utilize the capacity of the interconnect).

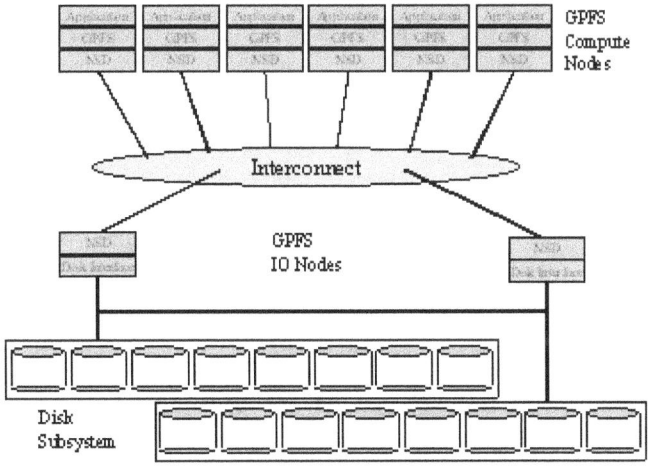

Figure 2-3: NSD Based GPFS Cluster

In a SAN simulation model, a subset of the cluster nodes is defined as GPFS I/O servers. The GPFS disk subsystem is only attached to the I/O servers. The NSD or VSD subsystem is responsible for the abstraction of disk data blocks across an IP-based interconnect. In such a configuration, the fact that the I/O requests are remote is transparent to the application that is issuing the file system calls. In Figure 2, a set of compute nodes is connected to a set of GPFS I/O servers via a high-speed interconnect. Each I/O server is attached to a portion of the disk subsystem. The recommendation made is that the disk subsystem is multi-tailed to the I/O servers for fail-over purposes. The choice of how many nodes to configure as I/O servers is based on the individual performance requirements and the capabilities of the storage subsystem, respectively. It has to be pointed out that in this model of storage attachment, it is not required to setup a complex SAN environment. Each storage solution is only attached to a small number of I/O servers (normally two), eliminating the necessity for (expensive) SAN switches [2].

The choice between a SAN attached or a SAN simulation model is performance and cost centric. The SAN simulation capabilities of GPFS provide economical solutions. In general, SAN subsystems provide the highest performance, but the cost and management complexity has to be considered when choosing such an approach. GPFS provides file data access from all the nodes in the cluster by providing a global name space for files. Applications can efficiently access files using standard UNIX file system interfaces, where GPFS supplies the data to any location in the cluster using the provided path to the storage. GPFS allows all the compute nodes that have the GPFS file system mounted to have coherent, as well as concurrent access to all of the storage (including write() sharing) resources. Some of the GPFS performance advantages are accomplished by (1) striping data across multiple disks that are attached to multiple nodes. (2) An efficient client side caching mechanism that includes read-ahead and write-behind techniques. (3) Utilizing a configurable block size, a feature that is especially important with some of the newer disk technologies where very large block sizes are paramount to aggregate storage performance. (4) Using block-level locking techniques that are based on a very sophisticated token management system that provides data consistency while allowing multiple application nodes to have concurrent access to the files.

Red Hat's Global File System (GFS)

Linux cluster technologies have become paramount to provide scalable performance and high availability. These services normally require that data can be shared among server nodes. Further, smaller companies often have many computer systems, including desktops and servers that may have to share data as well. Therefore, data sharing is a requirement for small, medium, and large companies, respectively. In general, static data (read only) can normally be split rather easily among server nodes. In such a scenario, each server node in the cluster may host a copy of the data set. However, in a dynamic data (read and write) environment that is rapidly changing, data replication is much more cumbersome. To address this issue, the basic idea of any parallel file system is that every server node in the cluster should have direct access to the data set, and that each server node should be able to read and write simultaneously.

GFS Version 3

Traditional local file systems support a persistent name space. A local file system views devices as being 'locally attached', the devices are not shared and so there is no need in the file system design to enforce 'device sharing' semantics. Instead, the focus is on aggressively caching and aggregating file system operations to improve performance by reducing the number of actual disk accesses required for each file system operation. New networking technologies allow multiple machines to share storage devices. GFS is a distributed file system that is taking a shared, network-attached storage approach. GFS is built on the premise that a shared disk file system has to exist within the context of a cluster infrastructure, and has to provide proper error handling and recovery, as well as the best performance possible. In a GFS environment, SAN clients only manage 'local file system requests' and act as 'file managers' for there own I/O operations. The storage devices serve the actual data directly to the clients. GFS utilizes 'callbacks' from clients requesting data that is being held exclusively by another client. The client holding the data (exclusively) releases it some time after the request. This paradigm implies direct client-to-client communication. Overall the design permits aggressive metadata and data caching which results in GFS performance that is comparable to local (Linux) file system performance. The GFS design provides transparent parallel access to storage devices while maintaining standard UNIX file system semantics. User applications only see a single logical device via the standard open, close, read, write and fcntl primitives. This transparency is important in regards to 'ease of use' as well as portability. The GFS design differs from traditional file systems, emphasizing sharing, connectivity, as well as caching. Unlike local file systems such as JFS or XFS, GFS distributes file system resources (including metadata) across the entire storage subsystem, which allows simultaneous access from multiple machines. In GFS version 3, Device Locks are the mechanisms that are being used to facilitate mutual exclusion of the file system metadata. Device Locks are further used to help maintain the coherence of the metadata when cached by several client nodes. The locks are implemented on the storage devices (the actual disks) and accessed via the SCSI device lock command dlock. The dlock command is independent of all other SCSI commands, so devices supporting the locks have no awareness of the nature of the resource that is locked. The GFS file system provides the mapping between the files and the dlock's.

To allow efficient recovery from failures, each GFS node writes to its own journal. When a GFS machine modifies metadata, than this process is recorded as a single transaction in that particular node's journal. If it fails, other machines notice that its locks have timed out, and one of the other nodes in the cluster will replay the failed machine's log and reboot the node. Other machines in the GFS cluster can continue accessing the file system as long as they do not have to access any metadata that can only be found in the failed client's journal. As an alternative to a disk-based locking design, GFS can also utilize a lock daemon that is running on any machine accessible to the GFS cluster over an IP network. Hence, special SCSI disks supporting the dlock firmware are not required to operate GFS. Further, GFS can be run without locks as a local file system solution. In GFS version 3, lock handling has been modularized so that GFS can utilize almost any globally accessible lock table. A Network Storage Pool (NSP) volume driver supports the abstraction of a single unified storage address space for the GFS nodes. The NSP is implemented in a device driver layer sitting atop of the basic SCSI device and Fibre Channel drivers. The NSP driver translates the logical request of the file system to the address space of each device.

GFS Version 4

In the GFS 4 version, the Device Memory Export Protocol (DMEP) is being used as a mechanism to synchronize client access to shared metadata. DMEP helps maintain metadata coherence when several clients access metadata. The dmep SCSI command allows a device to export memory to clients, and clients map the 'lock state' (which is either 'not held', 'held', or 'held & locked') into these memory buffers. The 'lock state' is contained in the storage devices (the actual disks) and accessed through the SCSI dmep command. As dlock in version 3, the dmep command that is being used in version 4 is independent of all other SCSI commands; devices supporting the locks have no awareness of the nature of the resource that is being locked (or even that the buffers are used to implement locks). The file system provides a mapping between file metadata and dmep buffers.

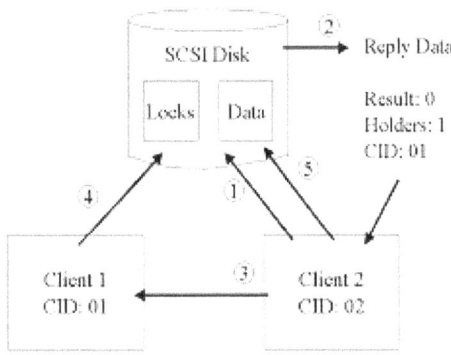

Figure 2-4: Callbacks on global locks in GFS

As already mentioned, GFS originally used the dlock SCSI command, which had the device maintaining the 'lock semantics' as well as the 'lock state'. The advantage of dmep over dlock is that the SCSI command is simpler, and the lock semantics may be modified on the client without affecting the SCSI command definition. All the semantics that used to be implemented by the SCSI devices as part of the dlock command are now implemented on the client. The dmep devices can be considered as just a reliable shared memory location. In version 4, the Pool Logical Volume Driver (PLVD) coalesces a heterogeneous collection of shared storage into a single logical volume. It was developed with GFS to provide simple logical device capabilities and to deliver dmep commands to specific devices at the SCSI driver layer. If GFS is used as a local file system where no locking is needed, then the PLVD is not required. GFS distributes its metadata throughout the network storage pool rather than focusing onto a single superblock solution. Multiple Resource Groups are used to partition the metadata into separate groups to increase file system scalability, to avoid bottlenecks, and to reduce the average size of a typical metadata search operation. One or more Resource Groups may exist on a single device or a single Resource Group may include multiple devices. Resource Groups are similar to the Block Groups that can be found in the Ext2 file system design. Like Resource Groups, Block Groups exploit parallelism and scalability by allowing multiple threads of a single system to allocate and free data blocks. The GFS Resource Groups allow multiple clients in the cluster to do the same.

The lock semantics used prior to GFS version 4 were tied directly to the SCSI dlock command. This tight coupling was unnecessary, as the lock usage in GFS could be abstracted so that GFS machines could exploit any global lock space available to all machines. GFS version 4 now supports an abstract lock module that can exploit almost any globally accessible lock space, not just dmep. This is important because it allows GFS cluster architects to purchase any disks, not only disks that contain the dmep firmware. A GFS lock module can implement callbacks to allow metadata caching and to improve lock acquisition latencies (as shown in Figure 1). For example, when Client 2 needs an exclusive lock that is already being held by Client 1, Client 2 sends first a regular dmep SCSI request to the disk drive (Step 1). This request fails and returns a list containing the 'lock holder', which in this case happens to be Client 1 (Step 2). In step 3, Client 2 sends an IP callback to Client 1, asking Client 1 to surrender the lock. Client 1 'syncs' the dirty data and metadata buffers associated with that lock to the disks (Step 4), and releases the lock. At that point, Client 2 may acquire the lock (Step 5).

In GFS, the implemented write cache methodology is write-back. GFS utilizes 'global locks' as well as interchangeable locking modules, some of which map the 'global locks' to dmep buffers (see Figure 2). The GFS design distinguishes among the following three lock states:

1. Not Held, which implies that the node does not hold the lock. Another node in the cluster may or may not hold the lock.

2. Held, which implies that the node is holding the lock, but that no current thread is utilizing the lock. Data buffered in the node's cache may not reflect the data on disk and there may be in-core transactions pending for that particular global lock. If another node requests that lock, the current lock holder will have to sync all the affected transactions and data buffers to disk prior to releasing the lock.

3. Held and Locked, which implies that the node holds the global lock and that there is an active thread using the lock. The data in the node's cache may or may not reflect the data on disk. If another node in the cluster requests the lock, the request is being ignored and acted upon later. The lock is not being released in GFS until the thread drops the 'lock state' down to the 'held state'.

In GFS (on a write request), the file system moves the global lock into the 'held & locked' state. At that point, the lock is acquired exclusively (if it is not already being held). As already discussed, if another thread is writing to that lock and the lock is in a 'held & locked' state, the second thread will have to wait until the lock is dropped to the 'held' state.

A write is being executed asynchronously. The actual I/O request is not necessarily written back to disk, the buffers are only marked as dirty and the lock state changes to 'held', which symbolizes the end of a write sequence. The buffers in memory remain marked dirty until either a 'bdflush' (Linux kernel thread) or sync operation occurs or another node in the cluster requests the lock. At that point, the transactions, as well as the data buffers, are synced to disk, the lock state changed to 'not held', and the lock is released. This design is imperative to the GFS performance, because it allows a node in the cluster to hold the lock until another node requests it. This allows a node to service multiple requests for the same lock without having to request a separate lock for every thread.

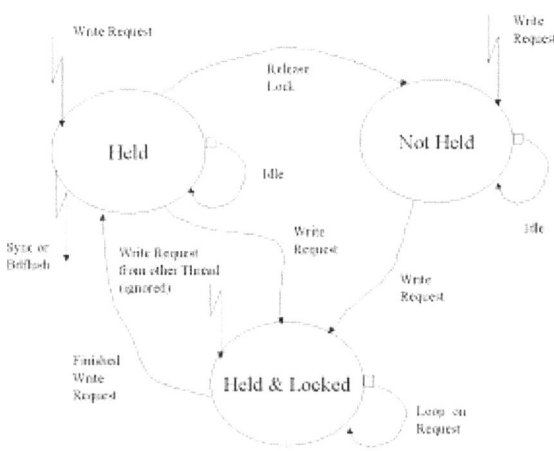

Figure 2-5: GFS Locks – STD

Further, GFS supports file system journaling. The GFS implementation is based on a 'Transaction' and a 'Log Manager' design. Journaling uses transactions for operations that change the metadata state. These operations must be atomic, so that the file system moves from one consistent on-disk state to another consistent on-disk state. These transactions generally correspond to vnode operations such as create, mkdir, write, or unlink. With transactions, the file system metadata can always be quickly returned to a consistent state. The Log Manager is separate from the transaction module. It takes metadata to be written from the transaction module and writes it to disk. The Transaction Manager pins, while the Log Manager unpins. The Log Manager also manages the 'Active Items List', and detects and deals with 'log wrap-around' situations. A GFS journaling transaction is composed of the metadata blocks changed during an atomic operation. Each journal entry has one or more locks associated with a particular transaction, corresponding to the metadata that is protected by a particular lock. As an example, a create() transaction contains locks for the directory, the new inode, as well as for the allocation maps. In GFS, all metadata blocks contain a 'generation number' that is incremented each time the metadata block is being changed. This mechanism is being used when a recovery operation is necessary. The steps involved and being executed by the Transaction Manager in creating a transaction can be defined as:

1. Start the transaction

2. Acquire the necessary global locks

3. Check conditions that are required for the transaction

4. Pin the in-core metadata buffers that are associated with the transaction

5. Modify the metadata in memory

6. Pass the global locks to the transaction

7. Commit the transaction by passing it to the Log Manager

Point 7 is achieved when Transaction Manager passes a structure containing a list of metadata buffers to the Log Manager. Each buffer is aware of its global lock number. Passing this structure basically represents a commit to the in-core log. To reiterate, the Transaction Manager pins the in-core metadata buffers whereas the Log Manger unpins the buffers. In GFS, each client has its own journal space that is protected by a single lock that is acquired at mount time and released when the file system is un-mounted. The in-core log entries are committed asynchronously to the disk log. The Log Manager executes the following steps:

1. Receives the transaction from the Transaction Manager

2. Stalls and combines transactions (asynchronous logging)

3. Performs the actual commit to disk

4. Moves the metadata into the Active Items List

5. Unpins the metadata in memory

6. Removes the metadata from the Active List as soon as the disk transaction is completed

	Lock 1	Lock 5	Lock 6	Lock 8	Lock 11
Transaction 1	X	X			
Transaction 2		X	X		
Transaction 3	X	X			
Transaction 4				X	X
Transaction 5					X

Figure 2-6: Lock Dependencies in GFS

All transactions in GFS are linked to one or more global locks. Other nodes in the cluster may request theses global locks during a 'callback operation'. The ramification is that callbacks may result in transactions being pushed out of the in-core log and written to the on-disk log file. Prior to surrendering a global lock, GFS has to:

1. Flush the transactions that depend on that particular global lock to the log file

2. Sync the metadata buffers

3. Sync the data buffers

The file system has to only flush the transactions that are either directly or indirectly dependent on the requested global lock. In GFS, a journal entry is dependent on a particular global lock if either it references that lock directly or it shares a lock (or even multiple locks) with other transactions that are referencing that particular lock directly.

To illustrate the process in Figure 2-6, five transactions are shown in sequential order, starting with transaction one. Further, Figure 2-6 shows the locks upon which each transaction is dependent on. Each 'X' represents an in memory metadata buffer that has to be written to disk. In this example, assuming lock six is requested by another node, transactions one, two, and three have to be flushed to the on-disk log file. In GFS, transactions that have overlapping locks are combined as they are committed to the in-core log and written to the on-disk log as a unit. The last step involves syncing the metadata and data buffers for lock six and to release the lock.

GFS Version 6 - Internals

The Global File System (GFS) was designed and developed as a 64-bit parallel file system solution. It enables several server nodes that are connected to a SAN to access a common, shared IO storage pool concurrently via standard POSIX file system semantics. GFS is a journaling file system. Each cluster node allocates its own journal. Changes to the file system metadata (the structural elements of the file system) are written into a journal. In case of a node failure, replaying the metadata operations out of the journal can restore file system consistency. Optionally, both data and metadata can be journaled [4].

GFS saves the file system descriptors in inode structures that are allocated dynamically (referred to as *dynamic nodes* or dinodes). The dinodes are placed inside a file system block (4KB reflects the standard file system block size in Linux). To reiterate, in a parallel file system environment, multiple server nodes access the file system concurrently, ergo the pooling of multiple dinodes in a single block would lead to an increased locking overhead and false sharing conditions. To address any potential space efficiency and to economize the number of disk access operations, file data may be stored in the dinode itself (if the file is small enough to fit inside a dinode). In this scenario, only one block access is necessary to load the file into memory. If the file is larger than a dinode, GFS utilizes a (traditional) flat file structure. All pointers in a dinode represent the same depth. GFS supports direct, indirect, and double indirect pointers. The height of the tree structure grows depending on the file size.

As in GPFS, an extendible hashing based approach is utilized to save the index structure for directories. For every filename a multi-bit hash value is saved as an index into the hash table. The corresponding pointer in the table represents a leaf node. Every leaf node can be referenced via multiple pointers. If a hash table leaf node becomes too small to save the directory entries, the size of the hash table is doubled. If one leaf node is too small, it splits itself up into two leaf nodes of the same size. If there are only a few directory entries in the file system, the directory information is saved within the dinode block itself. This data structure allows each directory search be performed in a number of disk accesses that is proportional to the depth of the extendible hashing tree structure (which is rather flat).

For very large directories with millions of files, only a small number of disk accesses are required to locate the directory entry. Further, GFS 6 offers new features such as file access control lists (ACL), quota, direct I/O, as well as on-the-fly (dynamic) enlargement of the file system.

GFS Version 6 - Layout

Figure 2-3 represents the basic layout of a typical GFS storage cluster solution. The GFS file system is mapped onto a IO subsystem pool, which is normally composed of several independent storage units. The server nodes are connected via a SAN infrastructure consisting of one or multiple data paths into the IO pool. The individual cluster server nodes are interconnected via one or more data paths in the network. Hence, every server node can directly access the IO storage solution, which increases I/O throughput and provides a scalability potential that is far beyond what can be achieved via a NAS server based solution.

The Linux operating system powers all the server nodes in a GFS storage cluster solution. A (rather simple) cluster volume manager (know as the GFS pool layer) virtualizes the storage units (/dev/sdx) and aggregates them into a single logical pool volume (dev/pool/name). Multiple IO devices can be combined via striping or concatenation. Any changes to the pool configuration are visible in the entire cluster. The pool volume manager allows resizing pool volumes on-the fly (online) and provides I/O multi-path capabilities, (which allows for single failure occurrences in the SAN path). However, the GFS pool volume manager does not provide volume mirroring or any snapshot capabilities. These features are provided via CLVM, the Cluster Logical Volume Manager, an LVM2-based cluster volume manager, which allows multiple server nodes to share access to a storage volume on a SAN.

The GFS lock server coordinates the access from the multiple server nodes to the same (physical) file system blocks in the storage cluster. The lock server provides (and enforces) actual file system data consistency. GFS was designed around a modular locking layer infrastructure. In earlier GFS versions, the lock information was exchanged via the SCSI protocol (DLOCK, DMEP). Since GFS version 5, a redundant, IP-based user space locking service (RLM), which is being executed on all the nodes, has been incorporated. Red Hat provides its distributed lock manager (DLM) for GFS 6.1 (2005). Each server node in the GFS cluster heartbeat's the lock server on a regular basis. If a server node is unable to heartbeat the lock manger, that node will be flagged by the lock manager and will be removed from the cluster setup (an operation known as fencing). GFS supports several fencing mechanisms such as different network power switch based solutions or Hewlett-Packards ILO interface.

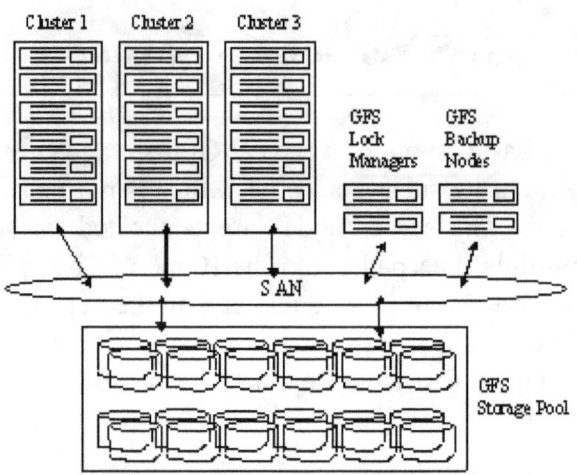

Figure 2-7: GFS storage cluster

GFS Version 6 – Scalability & Availability Considerations

A traditional IT system setup may consist of services and applications that are executed on individual server systems (in other words the applications are bound to a single server setup). If the application outgrows the capabilities of the server hardware, a capacity study normally recommends an (expensive) hardware upgrade. In contrast, applications that can run in parallel on a cluster are much easier to scale. In case of a capacity shortage, new (and mostly cheaper) components can easily be integrated into the system (until the capacity requirements are met). The common usage of the IO storage pool not only eliminates the need for (labor-intensive) data duplication scenarios, but also offers efficient scalability potentials. While encountering growing storage requirements, the common storage pool can easily be expanded and instantly be made available to the entire user community. To achieve availability requirements in the 99% to 99.9% uptime range, it is necessary to eliminate all potential single point of failure components. To achieve availability requirements in the 99.9% to 99.99% uptime range, it is required to setup an HA cluster, mirrored data capabilities, as well as a 2nd data center for disaster recovery. The applications have to have the possibility to run on multiple server nodes at different locations. The failure of one server or the entire data center must not avert the application accessibility more than a short period of time. SAN solutions that are connected via redundant I/O paths have the capability to survive individual component failure (such as cables, switches, or host bus adapters). An I/O multi-path solution can be implemented either via the Fibre channel driver for the host bus adapter, or via the GFS IO storage pool. Host-based mirroring in a GFS cluster is provided in GFS 6.1 via the Cluster Logical Volume Manager (CLVM) component. The lock server, whom is essential for GFS to operate, is available in two versions. There is a simple version (Single Lock Manager - SLM), which represents a single point of failure for the entire system, and a redundant version (Redundant Lock Manager - RLM). It is feasible (and recommended) to define multiple lock servers (via RLM). In such a scenario, a secondary lock manger can transparently take over the role of an active lock server. Further, Red Hat's Cluster Suite can be utilized to provide application fail-over capabilities in a GFS cluster environment.

GFS Version 6 - Backup Capabilities

A data backup is normally performed via backup client machines (which are production application servers in most setups). The backup is performed either via the LAN to a dedicated backup server (products like Legato Networker or Veritas Netbackup can be used), or in a LAN-free setup, from the application server directly to the backup devices. As every connected server node that is utilizing a parallel file system has access to the entire data pool, it is feasible to use a server node to be the backup server. It is further useful to generate snapshots (or clones) of GFS volumes by using the hardware snapshot capabilities of many storage products. These snapshot volumes can be mounted and backed up via a GFS backup server. To enable this feature, GFS provides a file system quiesce capability to ensure a consistent (data) state. In a nutshell, quiesce implies that all accesses to the file system are halted after a file system sync operation, which insures that all metadata and data is written to the storage unit (in a consistent state) prior to taking the snapshot [4].

Summary and Conclusion

This chapter introduced some of the terminology and features used in the world of cluster file systems. It has to be emphasized that the key components to be considered while planning for a cluster installation (and therefore choosing a cluster file system) are (1) scalability, (2) high performance, and (3) robust fail-over techniques. These features are definitely playing an increasingly important role in high performance cluster deployments, and not every cluster file system excels in all three areas.

References

1.	Cluster File Systems, "About the Lustre Architecture", Lustre File System, 2005

2.	IBM Corporation, "GPFS Primer for AIX Clusters", Boulder, 2005

3.	OSDL, "Cluster file system taxonomy", 2005

4.	Red Hat, "Red Hat Global File System", 2005

5.	Welch Brent, "What is a Cluster File System", 2005

6.	Abdelrahman T., Wong, T., "Distributed array data management on NUMA multiprocessors", In Proceedings of SHPCC, May 1994.

7.	Agarwal, A., Bianchini, B., Chaiken, D., Johnson, K., Kranz, D., "The MIT Alewife Machine: Architecture and Performance", Proceedings of the 21st Annual International Symposium on Computer Architecture, April 1995.

8.	Anderson J., Lam, M., "Global Optimization for Parallelism and Locality on Scaleable Parallel Machines", In Proceedings of the SIGPLAN'93 Conference on Programming Language Design and Implementation, June 1993.

9.	Balasundaram, V., Fox, G., Kennedy, K., Kremer, K., "A static performance estimator to guide data partitioning decisions", In Proceeding of 3rd ACM SIGPLAN Symposium on Principles and Practice of Parallel Programming, Williamsburg, Virginia, 1991.

10.	Blount, M., Butrico, M., "DSVM6K: Distributed Shared Virtual Memory on the RS/6000", Proceedings of the 38th Annual IEEE Computer Society International Computer Conference, Spring 1993.

11.	Cray Research GmbH, "The Cray Research Massively Parallel Processor System - Cray T3D", Munich, Germany, 1993.

12.   Hagersten, E., Landin, A., Haridi, S., "DDM - A Cache Only Memory Architecture", IEEE Computer, September 1992.

13.   Heinrich, M., Kuskin, J., "The Stanford FLASH Multiprocessor", In Proceeding of the 21st Annual International Symposium on Computer Architecture, 1994.

14.   Hennessy, J., Patterson, D., "Computer Architecture, a Quantitative Approach", Morgan Kaufmann Publishers, Third Edition, 2002

15.   Koenigs, A. *"Parallel Application Performance"*, Lawrence Livermore National Laboratory, 1998

16.   Koenigs, A. *"Industrial Strength Parallel Computing"*, Morgan Kaufmann, San Francisco, 2000

17.   Liberty, D., "Simple COMA Shared Memory and the RS/6000 SP", White Paper IBM RS/6000 Division, Austin, 1998

18. Martin, J., Agerwala, T., Mirza, D., Sadler, M., Snir, D., "SP2 system architecture", Scaleable Parallel Computing, Volume 34, 1995

19.   Reinhardt, S., Larus, J., Wood, D., "Tempest and Typhoon: User Level Shared Memory", Proceedings of the 21st Annual International Symposium on Computer Architecture, April 1994.

20.   Saman, P., Anderson, M., Lam, M., Lim, A., "An overview of a compiler for scaleable parallel machines", Languages and Compilers for Parallel Computing, Springer, 1993

21.   Schoinas, I., Falsafi, B., Lebeck, A., Reinhardt, S., Larus, J., Wood, D., "Fine-grain Access Control for Distributed Shared Memory", Proceedings of the Sixth International Conference on Architectural Support for Programming Languages and Operating Systems, October 1994.

22.   Shah, G., Nieplocha, J., Kim, C., Harrison, R., Gildea, K., DiNicola, P., Bender, C., "Performance Experience with LAPI", IPPS 98, International Parallel Processing Symposium, Orlando, FL, 1998

23.   Silcock, J., Goscinski, A.,"Update Based Distributed Shared Memory Integrated into RHODOS' Memory Management", Proc. of IEEE 3rd Int'l Conf. on Algorithms & Architectures for Parallel Processing (ICA3PP'97", 239--252, 1997.

24.   Sohda, y., Nakada, H., Matsuoka, S., Ogawa, H., "Implementation of a Portable Software DSM in Java", *ACM JavaGrande/ISCOPE 2001 Conference*, Jun. 2001.

25.   "The Sun Enterprise Cluster Architecture", Technical White Paper Sun Microsystems, Milpitas, CA, 1997

Chapter 3 – InfiniBand, SAN and NAS – Introduction, Performance, & Technology

Introduction

In 2000, a new high-speed interconnect (InfiniBand) was announced that could and would replace all the other internal and external system interconnects (or at least that was the goal). The announcement was met with overwhelming silence. Then, on the heels of the announcement came the burst of the dot-com bubble, and InfiniBand was seemingly left for dead. Thankfully, the InfiniBand community was able to outlast the slow adoption rate, and quietly developed a very robust solution. Today, InfiniBand is widely deployed and provides high-speed (from 10Gbit/sec., to 60Gbit/sec. and potentially up to 120Gbit/sec.) interconnects [2]. InfiniBand supports interconnections within or among servers (server-to-server connectivity), as well as among storage systems (server-to-storage and storage-to-storage connectivity).

Major corporations are now introducing InfiniBand based solutions. To illustrate, Sun Microsystems announced that SUN's Utility Computing Grid will be based on InfiniBand, and IBM has presented an InfiniBand based solution for the IBM blade center (in collaboration with Topspin). Further, IBM supports InfiniBand for their General Parallel File System (GPFS) based clusters. In addition, SGI, integrated InfiniBand in its Altix servers. The user community can now take advantage of the provided InfiniBand features such as high bandwidth, extremely low latency periods, simple implementation, and low costs to build sound cluster interconnects or robust SAN solutions.

InfiniBand - Definition

InfiniBand represents a high-performance, switch-based interconnect architecture that is designed to operate within a server (component-to-component communication, replacing existing bus technologies), as well as an external interconnect solution (frame-to-frame communication for server or storage components). It offers a single interconnect for clustering, communication and storage purposes. Some of InfiniBand's key benefits are:

- Backed by industry standards, basically in the same way as T11 is responsible for the Fibre Channel standards, and the Internet Engineering Task Force (IETF) is looking over the iSCSI and Internet standards, the InfiniBand Trade Association is governing the InfiniBand standards.

- Max performance with minimal latency overhead. The current InfiniBand specification ranges from 10Gbit/sec. to 60G bit/sec. with very minimal latency overhead, which is typically measured in nanoseconds. To illustrate, nanoseconds are also used to measure read() and write() access times to physical memory.

- The InfiniBand *hardware transport* implements communication functionality's (that are traditionally performed by an operating system and the CPU) in the firmware of the InfiniBand device. This drastically reduces CPU overhead, and allows the host processor to allocate its CPU cycles to the user applications rather than on communication entities.

- Remote Direct Memory Access (RDMA). This capability allows systems to transfer data in main memory without involving the processor, cache or operating system of either compute node. RDMA transfers drastically reduce CPU overhead and again, allow the CPUs to spend their cycles serving application requests and not having to process communication requests.

InfiniBand – Usage & Application

Besides enabling higher performance within a server (replacing PCI buses with InfiniBand fabrics), InfiniBand introduces bandwidth capacities that are normally used for CPU-to-CPU and CPU-to-memory communications outside of the server. It allows physically separated systems to comunicate with each other as if they would represent a single, large symmetric multiprocessing system. Traditional application clusters, such as Oracle RAC, rely on proprietary interconnects or TCP/IP to manage the complex nature of the inter-cluster traffic. The slow inter-process communication mechanism among the server nodes limits most cluster sizes to only a few nodes, as the overhead of a distributed lock manager on an active cluster may cause the database processes to take a significant performance hit.

TCP/IP over Gigabit Ethernet (GigE) introduces a rather significant load on the CPU (next to providing a limited bandwidth and higher latency than InfiniBand). Each additional node in the cluster introduces more overhead and traffic, limiting the aggregate performance potential of the cluster. IP-over-InfiniBand (IPoIB) eliminates this bottleneck. Application servers communicating with the cluster have similar issues. TCP/IP communications with the cluster may have a negative impact on performance (this is of course workload based). It is hard to justify a high-performance cluster setup if the application servers have only limited access (performance wise) to the data. InfiniBand connections between the cluster and the application servers eliminate the bottleneck [1],[3].

The RDMA feature of InfiniBand, using the Message Passing Interface (MPI), allows database servers in the cluster to directly read and write to each other's memory. This eliminates the TCP/IP and operating system overhead, which increases (1) the performance of each node and (2) the aggregate performance of the entire cluster. The IPoIB inter-processor communication allows the cluster to work on a single application similar to a large SMP system, without the notorious scalability issues fond on SMP systems. Many of today's servers require three different network adapters to efficiently and effectively operate. (1) A GigE card for the LAN, (2) a Fibre Channel card for the SAN, and (3) a dedicated server-to-server clustering card (either proprietary or another GigE card). And in some instances, the cluster nodes may require an additional dedicated GigE card to connect to a backup network. In a blade server environment, providing each blade system with 3 cards introduces some issues, including increased power consumption, additional space requirements within the server, higher costs, greater complexity, and an increased heat issue. A blade server with an InfiniBand backplane eliminates the three cards. The backplane further enables RDMA capabilities to allow the blade servers to act as one unit (if necessary).

The adoption of InfiniBand in blade server systems and cluster solutions has been growing for some time. Clusters are designed to cost-effectively provide massive processing power. To truly deliver on that, they have to have high-performance and low-latency communication features (especially to the storage components). In order for InfiniBand-based cluster systems to utilize high-performance Fibre Channel storage, enhanced solutions have to be developed [2]. One solution is to create a separate Fibre Channel SAN. And even though SAN bandwidth has recently doubled to 4Gbit/sec., separate Fibre Channel switches and host adapters create multiple network fabrics, increasing the cost and the complexity. The other option is an InfiniBand-to-Fibre Channel gateway.

Such a solution has its drawbacks though. Gateways can become a performance bottleneck, they still are rather expensive, and they increase latency due to added protocol translation scenarios. As a result, the next step in the InfiniBand evolution is to tackle the storage subsystems. Native InfiniBand interfaces enable storage systems to attach directly to the existing InfiniBand fabric switches that are in use by the cluster, simplifying the network, and providing significant cost savings compared to Fibre Channel or gateway based solutions [1]. Additionally, native InfiniBand interfaces require no InfiniBand-to-Fibre Channel protocol translations (within the controller), enabling higher performance and lower latency scenarios. InfiniBand's high (per-channel) bandwidth (which is more than double the 4Gbit/sec. Fibre Channel bandwidth) delivers maximum throughput across a minimum number of InfiniBand connections. This saves on switch ports and lowers the acquisition and service costs, respectively.

SAN & NAS Solutions

At a first glance, SAN and NAS solutions seem almost identical, and as a matter of fact, many times either solution may be applicable in any given environment. In general, NAS and SAN solutions utilize RAID systems that are connected to an interconnect (network) [4],[6]. However, there are *significant differences* between SAN & NAS solutions, which do have a profound impact on how the actual data is being accessed and utilized (see Figure 3-1). Most SAN verses NAS comparisons focus on the actual wires, but the argument can be made that the protocols are the most important factor that distinguish the two solutions. To illustrate, one thesis is that SCSI is faster than Ethernet, and hence reflects a better solution from a performance perspective [4]. This statement is normally based on that fact that the TCP/IP overhead significantly impacts the efficiency of any data transfer scenario.

The Wires being used:

- NAS solutions utilize TCP/IP based networks, such as Ethernet, FDDI, or ATM
- SAN solutions use Fibre Channel connections

The Protocols being used:

- NAS solutions use TCP/IP and NFS/CIFS/HTTP based networks

- SAN solutions utilizes Fibre Channel encapsulated SCSI setups

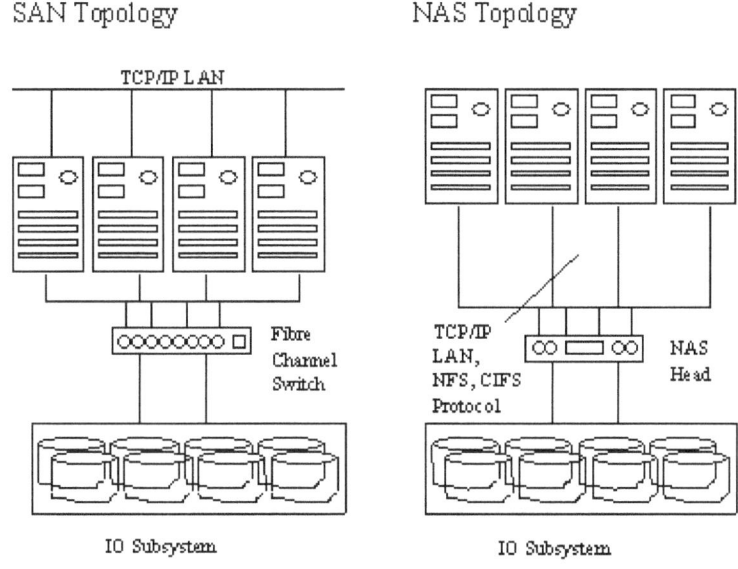

Figure 3-1: SAN & NAS Topology

Table 3-1: Additional SAN NAS Differences

NAS	SAN
Almost any machine that connects to a LAN (or is interconnected to a LAN via a WAN) may utilize NFS, CIFS or HTTP protocol to connect to a NAS	Server class devices that are equipped with SCSI Fibre Channel adapters connect to a SAN. A Fibre Channel based solution has a distance limit of approximately 6 miles

A NAS identifies the data by file name and byte offset, transfers file data or metadata, and handles security, user authentication, file locking	A SAN addresses the data by logical block numbers, and transfers the data in (raw) disk blocks.
A NAS allows greater sharing of information, especially among different operating systems	File Sharing is operating system dependent, and may not exist for all operating systems that are being used
File system is managed by the NAS head unit	The SAN servers manage the file system
Backups and mirrors are generated on files, not blocks (this may save bandwidth and time)	Backups and mirrors require a block by block copy operation. A mirrored system has to be either identical, or greater in capacity (compared to the source)

NAS Terminology

- The NAS head represents the part of the NAS solution required for the clients to connect to the IO subsystem. Behind the NAS head, hundreds or thousands of GB of available IO storage may exist, but the clients have to access the IO space via the NAS head. A NAS head is also called a NAS Gateway (a system), which serves as the actual control function of a NAS

- NFS (Network File System) is one of the communications protocols usually supported by NAS heads (for the communication with the network clients); particular in UNIX or Linux based solutions. It has to be pointed out though that NFS clients are available for just about any operating systems these days

- The CIFS (Common Internet File System) protocol is primarily responsible for file sharing and communication with Windows (and Linux-based Samba) servers, and represents another commonly supported protocol for most NAS heads. Most Windows clients utilize CIFS to communicate with the NAS head. Both, NFS and CIFS utilize TCP/IP as the underlying communication facility.

SAN Terminology

- A SAN solution can be loosely described as a network of storage disks. In large environments, a SAN connects multiple server systems to a centralized pool of disk storage. Compared to managing hundreds of servers (each with its own disk subsystem), SAN's simplify system administration tasks. By treating all the company's storage as a single resource, disk maintenance and backups are easier to schedule and control.

- SAN solutions provide high-speed disk access capabilities. The SAN network allows data transfers among server systems and IO subsystems at the same (high peripheral channel) speeds, as if the IO subsystems were directly attached to the serve systems. The Fibre Channel technology is the driving force behind SAN's, and is typically used to encapsulate SCSI commands. SSA and ESCON channels are also supported in SAN environments [5].

- The question of centralized or distributed solution may arise in a SAN design study. A centralized SAN connects multiple server systems to a collection of disks, whereas a distributed SAN typically uses one or more Fibre Channel or SCSI switches to connect the nodes from several buildings or campuses. For longer distances, SAN traffic may be transferred across ATM or SONET fabrics

- SAN over IP. Another valuable SAN option is an IP storage based solution, which enables data transfers via IP over fast Gigabit Ethernet (locally) or via the Internet (remotely).

- A Channel Attached verses Network Attached discussion may surface in the SAN/ NAS design phase as well. The NAS solution reflects basically a file server solution that attaches to the LAN (like any other node on the network). Rather than supporting a full-blown operating system, a NAS utilizes a slim micro-kernel that is specialized to handle only file reads and writes (CIFS, NFS, and NCP). However, a NAS may be subject to the variable performance behavior and overhead scenarios of a network that may contain and serve thousands of users.

SAN & Fibre Channel

Fibre Channel (FC) solutions reflect point-to-point, serial bi-directional interfaces. *4G Fibre Channel solutions will replace 1G and 2G storage networks in the near future.* The current technology used in Fibre Channel SANs reflects the 2G technology, which allows for a maximum throughputs of up to 2 Gbps. However, as demand for bandwidth-intensive applications (such as CAD/CAM, real-time computing, data warehousing or video streaming) grows, this speed will be insufficient, and hence has to be increased [6]. That is where 4G Fibre Channel solutions emerge, a technology, which doubles the maximum throughput to 4 Gbps. The new specs for 4G were approved by FCIA (Fibre Channel Industry Association) in 2003, and it is widely supported by most vendors today. Originally, the specs sought to deal with internal connectivity, connecting disk drives to the server [8]. Later it was decided to extend it for interconnecting the switching Fabric in SAN solutions. This basically includes the Fibre Channel switches, which intelligently manage the interconnectivity among various devices and nodes in a SAN. The 4G technology maintains backward compatibility with both older specs (1G and 2G). It also supports the loop architecture that is common to both older solutions. Customers can incrementally upgrade their systems to 4G. The technology reduces the number of connections among IO storage systems and server nodes, while significantly improving the throughput (this is workload dependent of course) [7].

4G products are starting to become more and more of a mainstream solution. Cisco focuses on their MSD 9000 family, whereas PMC-Sierra produces some of the 4G switches. Emulex has its HBA's (Host Bus Adapters) and embedded storage switches benchmarked and tested for 4G. Broadcom has launched the BCM 8421 repeater for 4G switches and storage arrays. Customers with high performance computing needs may find the technology useful, as faster backups and data recovery can be performed. Scientific environments that need to access large amounts of data to solve complex problems have the opportunity to take advantage of a 4G Fibre Channel solution as well. High quality graphics, such as animated movies, can be produced in lesser time [9]. The 4G technology also offers reliable transmission of digital audio/video applications. It has to be pointed out though, that at the moment, a significant number of customers are not taking full advantage of the existing 1 Gbps and 2 Gbps Fibre-Channel solutions. Fibre Channel is rather expensive to set up (especially for smaller environments) and hence, iSCSI may be a valuable alternative. It has to be reemphasized though that iSCSI is not as fast as a Fibre Channel based solution.

Summary

In a nutshell, NAS devices are storage appliances, large, single-purpose servers that plug into a network. These appliances perform one task, and they do it well. The capacity of large NAS appliances is typically in the TB range, while SAN solutions reflect multi-server multi-storage networks that may grow to hundreds of TB's. A SAN acts as a secondary network to a LAN, and every connected server that requires access to the SAN has to have a Fibre Channel connection to the SAN. Another key distinction between NAS and SAN solutions is the concept of heterogeneous file sharing. NAS appliances define heterogeneity at the file or data-block level, while SAN solutions normally define heterogeneity at the volume level. Out of the box, a NAS appliance allows UNIX and Windows clients to share the same file. In a SAN, a storage system, not that actual data, is shared. The storage is shared at the cabinet level by partitioning a physical storage device, assigning logical volumes to a given server. In most cases, a Windows server is prevented from accessing a UNIX volume and vice versa. Both methods allow performing data backups and restores, each providing their own benefits. In a NAS environment, a client makes a file system call over the network, as opposed to execute device-oriented commands from a server to a storage device in a SAN setup.

References

1. Alfaro, Sanchez, Duato, Das. "A Strategy to Compute the InfiniBand Arbitration Tables". In Int'l Parallel and Distributed Processing Symposium, April 2002.

2. Jni, "Introduction to InfiniBand" Jni Corporation, 2003

3. Liu, Wu, Panda, "High Performance RDMA-Based MPI Implementation over InfiniBand", Ohio State University, 2004

4. Joachim, "Storage Pipeline: A Look at the Storage Professional," Network Computing, 16 September 2004..

5. Menon, Pease, Rees, Duyanovich, Hillsberg, "IBM Storage Tank—A heterogeneous scalable SAN file system," IBM Systems Journal, July 2003.

6. Shepler, Callaghan, Robinson, Thurlow, Beame, Eisler, Noveck, "Network File System (NFS) version 4 Protocol", IETF RFC 3530, April 2003.

7. Benner. "Fibre channel: Gigabit Communications and I/O for Computer Networks". McGraw-Hill, 1996

8. Ruwart. "Performance Characterization of Large and Long Fibre Channel Arbitrated Loops". Mass Storage Systems, 1999. IEEE Symposium, 1999

9. Heath, Yakutis. "High-Speed Storage Area Networks Using a Fibre Channel Arbitrated Loop Interconnect". IEEE Network, 2000

Chapter 4 - A Cohesive Framework to Quantify Computer Systems Assurance

Introduction

This chapter introduces a system-engineering and evaluation methodology that focuses on the stability of an entire computing infrastructure. More specifically, the conducted research elaborates on the cohesive systems assurance (CSA) methodology, which encapsulates the concepts and methods of 1) product assurance (reliability, availability, and maintainability), 2) performance & scalability, and 3) dependability (security and safety). The argument made in this study is that systems stability represents the *quality of service* provided by an entire computing infrastructure, and therefore quantifies the usefulness, trustworthiness, and effectiveness of the environment.

This chapter bases the motivation for CSA (cohesive systems assurance) on the thesis that the interrelationships among the dimensions of systems stability are paramount to the overall acceptance of a computing infrastructure by the user community. The proposed approach allows quantifying the cohesive stability aspects of an entire infrastructure by scrutinizing and analyzing the interrelationships among the stability dimensions. This approach substantially deviates from the pervasive systems engineering and analysis process in use today, which treats each of the dimensions of product assurance, performance and scalability, and dependability individually in a vacuum. The proposed CSA methodology can be utilized to quantify the relative impact that potential design alternatives may have on the overall infrastructure stability. The study first introduces the dimensions of CSA, and secondly elaborates via an actual case study on the pragmatic aspects of the methodology.

The CSA Equation

In the CSA methodology, the systems assurance dimensions (product assurance, performance & scalability, and dependability) are all components of the *CSA equation*. In this architecture, the product assurance component is decomposed into availability, reliability, and maintainability. The dependability component employs the security and safety issues, whereas the performance & scalability dimension discuss the traditional performance aspects of the entire infrastructure. The term *systems assurance* introduced in this paper is loosely based on *product assurance*, a term that is being used in Operations Research [10]. The argument made is that while systems assurance considerations are paramount in basically all acquisition projects, it reflects a much more involved framework for larger systems acquisitions, acquisitions of complex systems, and acquisitions of systems with significant support requirements.

The CSA equation reflects a *figure of merit* that allows identifying the component(s) that detract from the overall stability of an entire infrastructure, and ergo depict(s) the greatest potential for improvements. Each component of the CSA equation is expressed as a probability value. The CSA equation can be used as a communication tool among the project teams. The newly proposed CSA equation is considered as a significant evolution of the *effectiveness equation* as described by Blanchard [3], Pecht [11], Landers [10], or Barringer [2] et al. The argument made is that the effectiveness equation only considers the availability, reliability, maintainability, and capability components, and therefore omits any potential scalability, security, and safety issues that may have a profound impact on the overall stability of an entire computing environment. To reiterate, the CSA equation (vector) proposed in this study is comprised of:

- *CSA stability = availability * reliability * maintainability * security * safety * performability*

In some circumstances, only a subset of the discussed dimensions has to be used to quantify the stability of a system. Utilizing the CSA equation leads the analyst through a very pragmatic process that incorporates analyzing all aspects of *systems stability*, by elaborating on the interrelationships among the different dimensions (see Figure 4-1). The CSA equation can be utilized to identify areas for improvements and to conduct cross infrastructure comparisons. Quantifying the elements of the CSA equation yields a comprehensive analysis tool that elaborates on the relative stability aspects of any potential design alternatives. Overall, the stability of an infrastructure is expressed as a value between 0 and 1 (0% to 100%).

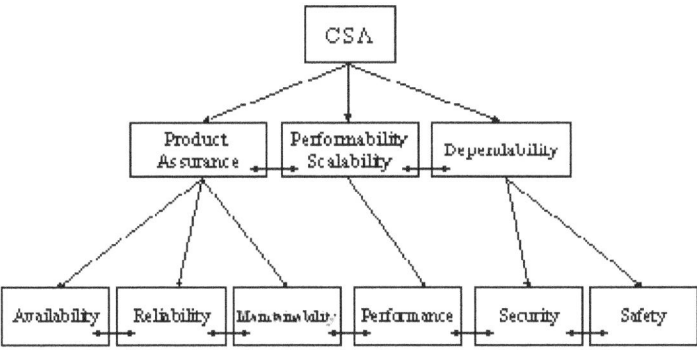

Figure 4-1: CSA Architecture

Each element used to construct the CSA equation consists in itself of a probability value that is defined in a range between 0 and 1. It is imperative to point out that in any computing environment, dependability and performance related issues depict an actual exercise in compromises that has to be taken into consideration when conducting a stability analysis. To reiterate, the thesis made in this study is that CSA engineering is not described as the *quest for perfection,* but rather the search for effective business solutions that provide a very high level of quality of service to the user community.

CSA – Product Assurance

Product Assurance describes the extent to which a mission critical computing environment is trusted by its user community, and represents the concepts and interrelationships among availability, reliability, and maintainability [10],[11]. In other words, product assurance can be described as a (qualitative) term that revolves around the ability of a computing infrastructure to *perform appropriately*.

Reliability Dimension

The reliability $R(t1)$ represents the probability that an environment operates correctly throughout a time interval *[t0,t1]*, given that the infrastructure was performing correctly at time *t0*. The reliability dimension is normally expressed in terms of the mean time between failure (MTBF) for repairable entities, and the mean time to failure (MTTF) for non-repairable entities, respectively. Reliability and availability are closely related terms, but it has to be emphasized that they do not depict interchangeable entities per se, as they represent different expressions revolving around the same issue [1]. To reiterate, reliability is focused on failure rate based statistics, whereas availability represents the measure of time a system or application component is operational [10].

Maintainability Dimension

The Maintainability *M(t)* represents the probability that a failed system component will be restored in order to resume processing within a time period *t*. The maintainability dimension represents an important component in mission critical environments where system faults might be introduced into the infrastructure during regular maintenance cycles. In other words, maintainability quantifies the *ease of repair* issue after a failure has been discovered, and concerns itself with system change scenarios such as the introduction of new application features.

In most circumstances, the key *figure of merit* for quantifying the maintainability of a system is the mean time to repair (MTTR), as well as a limit for the maximum repair time [4]. Qualitatively, maintainability refers to the ease with which any software or hardware component can be restored to a functional state. The MTTR component includes corrective maintenance, which consists of fault isolation and correction procedures. Quantitatively, maintainability is expressed as another probability value.

Availability Dimension

The availability *A(t0)* represents the probability that a given system or environment is operating correctly at the instant of time *t0*, and is normally expressed in terms of the mean time between failure (MTBF) and the mean time to repair (MTTR) components, respectively [10]. As MTBF and MTTR represent the reliability and maintainability dimensions, respectively, the availability dimension depicts an actual link between the two characteristics.

CSA - Dependability

Security Dimension

The security aspect of an environment is considered as an infrastructure property that reflects the environment's ability to withstand accidental or deliberated attacks. Security is an essential prerequisite for availability, reliability, and safety and has a profound impact on systems and application performance [12],[13]. In terms of the stability equation, security *S(t1)* represents the probability that a system does withstand accidental or deliberated attacks in a time interval *[t0,t1]*, given the fact that the infrastructure was secured up to an agreed upon *security standard* at time *t0*. As an example, the security dimension might be expressed as the mean time to security failure (MTTSF) [13]. A less complex approach than what is being discussed in [13] revolves around assigning a security probability in respect to the presence or absence of certain best-practice based functional characteristics, as well as development and configuration techniques. As security aspects have a profound impact on the performability dimension, the recommendation is (if feasible) to combine the two studies into one construct.

This author believes that it is imperative to shift the industry away from only restricting access to information and towards actively permitting access to different levels of information in an environment that is considered secure. Further, decomposing autonomous segments of the IT infrastructure into secure regions allows further hardening an environment. As already discussed, the concept of security can be described as an exercise in compromises. The compromises revolve around the question of how much loss of functionality and performance an organization is able to sacrifice in order to achieve an acceptable level of security that still allows the business to operate in an effective and efficient manner.

Safety Dimension

The safety aspect of an entire infrastructure can be described as the environmental property of the system's ability to operate, either normally or abnormally without the danger of causing human injury or death, or any other damage to the environment. Safety, availability, and reliability concerns are related issues that have to be analyzed accordingly. In terms of the stability equation, the safety *ST(t1)* represents the probability that a system does not cause any catastrophic effects in a time interval *[t0,t1]*, given that the environment was considered as being safe at time *t0*.

It has to be pointed out that a system might be unreliable but safe [12]. Hence, reliability and availability are considered as being necessary but not sufficient to guarantee safety. Reliability is concerned with conformance to a given specification, whereas safety is concerned with ensuring an environment does not cause any damage irrespective of any conformance to a given specification.

CSA – Performability/Scalability

In any contemporary computing environment, the motivation for parallel processing is based on the economics of scale offered by an efficiently used parallel infrastructure [6] [7]. This author argues that any scalability model is impacted by serialization and coherency factors that have a profound impact on overall systems performance. Algorithmic constraints play a decisive role in determining the amount of parallelism, and therefore the degree of scalability that is possible for any given application environment. The computational overhead encountered in any parallel environment can be defined as the fraction of CPU capacity that can not be utilized to process a certain workload [5],[6]. This behavior diminishes the potential economics of scale offered by the already-discussed parallel environment.

The multithreaded application, the workload and its distribution, the operating system, as well as the underlying hardware impact any performance study conducted in a parallel environment. The *performance focus* has to be on the interrelationship among the components. In regards to the stability equation, the performability /scalability *P(pt1,t1)* represents the probability that aggregate systems performance/scalability will be at or even above a certain performance/scalability level *pt1* in a time interval *[t0,t1]*, given that the environment was performing at or above a performance/scalability level *pt0* at time *t0*.

CSA – Methodology & Case Study

The proposed CSA architecture supports a comprehensive, decomposition-based methodology that follows a divide-and-conquer approach (see Figure 1). Utilizing the CSA architecture results into applying a very pragmatic analysis approach that incorporates the interrelationships and trade-off' among all the aspects of the application and systems components that compose the environment (see Figure 2).

The dimensions of CSA (or a subset thereof) are regarded as the individual input components into the CSA equation that is being used as a communication facility among the involved parties. The resulting CSA factor (a value between 0 and 1) can be utilized to:

- Quantify the relative stability of an entire computing environment

- Conduct a comprehensive cross infrastructure comparison

- Evaluate design alternatives

- Identify potential areas for improvement

- Communicate relative systems stability issues and concerns in a simple, but very effective manner

Table 1 outlines the CSA data as determined on three large-scale UNIX-based SMP database servers. The conducted study focused on product assurance, performability, as well as dependability. To determine the reliability, maintainability, availability, and performance factors, an analytical modeling based approach was utilized [4],[8]. Further, as the database systems were available for this study, an empirical performance and security analysis was conducted in all three environments. Quantifying the security factor was accomplished by assigning a security probability to the presence or absence of certain best-practice based functional characteristics, as well as development and configuration techniques.

Table 1: CSA Data – SMP Database Servers

CSA	DBS-1	DBS-2	DBS-3
Reliability	0.9933	0.9923	0.9928
Maintainability	0.999	0.896	0.997
Availability	0.99997	0.99992	0.99994
Performance	0.93	0.91	0.92
Security	0.93	0.94	0.95
CSA Factor	0.858	0.76	0.865

The product assurance model implemented for this study combines the probability that a system will perform its required functions for the duration of a specified time interval, and that the repair action under given conditions of use is carried out within a stated time interval as. Historical data, as well as data provided by the hardware vendors was utilized to calibrate the models. The reliability and maintainability was determined by using a Weibull-based analysis technique, whereas availability was determined based on MTBF and MTTR data [4],[8],[9].

Normalizing the stability data across infrastructures has to be conducted by applying the *same rules and guidelines* for all the dimensions that are being quantified. In brief, the importance of quantifying elements of the CSA equation is to identify potential areas for improvements. While conducting the analysis, it is paramount to take the interrelationships among the dimensions into consideration. As an example, any security related guidelines have a profound impact on systems performance, and hence a security and performance analysis should be conducted as a unit, and should not be performed by isolating the security from the performance aspects. The same philosophy holds true for any potential availability, reliability, and performance standards that have to be met in a given computing environment. The data in Table 1 represents the three independent computing environments (SMP UNIX based database servers) that were being scrutinized and compared from a relative CSA perspective. The goals were to (1) identify potential areas of improvements and (2) to determine which infrastructure provides the greatest CSA potential. The data reveals that the two systems DBS-1 and DBS-3 have an almost identical CSA value, whereas DBS-2's CSA value is substantially lower. At first glance, all three infrastructures indicate the potential for improvements in the areas of performance and security. Further, the data in Table 1 disclose a rather low maintainability factor for DBS-2. The analysis revealed a logistical problem in that environment, and an additional Weibull simulation conducted for this study was used to communicate the availability behavior (see Figure 4-3).

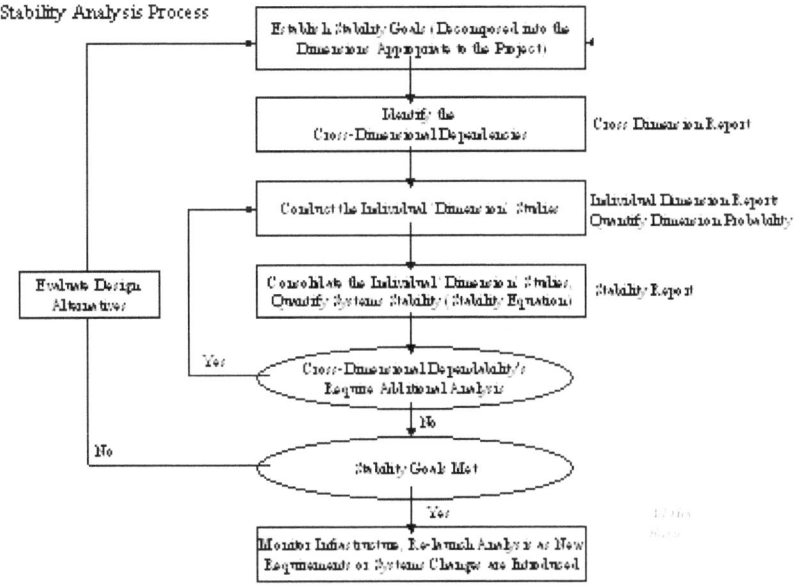

Figure 4-2: CSA Analysis Process

By addressing the rather low maintainability behavior, the potential of increasing the overall CSA factor for DBS-2 is striking. The model revealed that lowering the MTTR component from 28 time-units down to 20 time-units would increase the maintainability factor to 0.9989 (from 0.896). Implementing this change would raise the overall CSA value for DBS-2 from 0.76 to 0.847, thus is basically in line with the two other infrastructures. While in circumstances such as this, improving the maintainability may be the right step, the potential impact on the other CSA dimensions has to be analyzed and quantified as part of the overall analysis (see Figure 4-2).

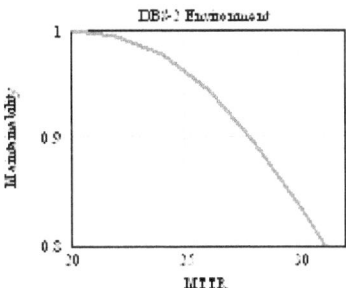

Figure 4-3: Maintainability Behavior – DBS-2

The thesis made in this study is that the current system analysis process overstates systems stability, as the dimensions are quantified individually in a vacuum. In a worst case scenario, aggregate systems stability is not even being addressed. From a business perspective, the current state of systems analysis can be considered as financially inefficient. The un-quantified systems and software stability issues have to be extensively analyzed and troubleshoot while the systems are in production.

CSA reduces the danger of analyzing the different systems dimensions in a vacuum, and therefore represents a technique that approximates reality as perceived by the user community. The focus of CSA is on the interrelationships among the dimensions, resulting into a comprehensive analysis that allows quantifying the relative Quality of Service provided by the computing infrastructure. Some of the cross-dimensional dependencies that have to be analyzed and quantified include:

- Error detection and recovery mechanisms (hardware and software related)

- Security aspects such as process accounting, transaction logging, and network (stack) tunables

- High availability and fault tolerance (environmental) aspects

- Performance enhancement techniques

- Hardware and software upgrades

- Workload changes and adjustments

- Effects of maintenance and service

The methodology's decomposition-based approach allows different project teams to conduct individual dimension oriented studies, but guides the analysts through a well-defined (iterative/perpetual) consolidation process. The ramification is a well understood and documented computing environment, where an organization is prepared for any contingency, resulting into an overall infrastructure that is from a financial, as well as a technical perspective, *manageable*.

Summary

The CSA architecture (or more specifically the elements that comprise the CSA equation) points toward the systems components where ample potential is available *to be explored*. The CSA methodology introduces a synergy effect into the standard systems analysis process that benefits from evaluating the interrelationships among the different dimensions. This in turn results in a profoundly improved infrastructure stability behavior. The modular design of the CSA architecture allows choosing the granularity of the stability analysis on a *per-project* basis. The emphasis in CSA is not on effective, but rather relative stability concerns. CSA does not pursue a quest for perfection, but rather seeks for efficient and affordable business oriented solutions that resolve the most pressing stability concerns in any computing environment.

References

1.   Barringer, H., Weber, D., "Where Is My Data For Making Reliability Improvements", 4th International Conference on PP Reliability, Houston, TX, 1995

2.   Barringer, H. Weber, P., "Life Cycle Cost Tutorial", 5th International Conference on PP Reliability, Houston, TX, 1996

3.   Blanchard, B. S., Dinesh V., Peterson, E., "Maintainability: A Key to Effective Serviceability and Maintenance Management", Prentice-Hall, Englewood Cliffs, NJ, 1997

4.   Gross, D., Harris, C., "Queuing Theory, Second Edition, Wiley, 1998

5.   Heger, D., Johnson, S., Anand, M., Peloquin, M., Sullivan, M., Theurer, M., Wong. P., "An Application Centric Performance Evaluation of the Linux 2.6 Operating System", IBM Red Book White Paper, Austin, TX, 2004

6.   Heger D., Simco G., "Quantifying the Cluster Speedup Behavior in the Realm of Internode Communication", Proceeding of the IEEE Southeast Conference, Fort Lauderdale. April 2005

7.   Hennessy, J., Patterson, D., "Computer Architecture, a Quantitative Approach", Third Edition, Morgan Kaufmann, 2002.

8.   Jain, R., "The Art of Computer System Performance Analysis", John Wiley, 1991

9.   Koenigs, A. "Industrial Strength Parallel Computing", Morgan Kaufmann, San Francisco, 2000

10.   Landers, R., "Product Assurance Dictionary", Marlton Publishers, Marlton, NJ, 1997

11. Pecht, M., "Product Reliability, Maintainability, and Supportability", CRC Press, NY, 1996

12. Schuster, S. "Security with Compromise", Analog Devices, 2005

13. Vaidyanathan K., Madan, B., Goseva, K., Trivedi, K., "A Method for Modeling and Quantifying the Security Attributes of Intrusion Tolerant Systems", DARPA, 2003

Chapter 5 - Modeling Based Performance Engineering

Introduction

The first part of this chapter elaborates on the vicious cycle of systems performance tuning and IT operational costs. In today's parallel, heterogeneous, and interconnected IT landscape, predicting and controlling the cost factors surrounding systems performance and capacity planning may seem overwhelming to many organizations. For larger IT projects, it is not uncommon to experience scenarios where the cost factors for performance tuning and capacity planning reflect the largest and the least controlled expenses. To illustrate, a sudden slowdown of an enterprise wide application may trigger user complaints, delayed projects, an IT support backlog, and ultimately a financial loss to the organization. By the time the performance problem is located, analyzed, worked around, tested, and verified, an organization may have spent tens of thousands of dollars in time, IT resources, and hardware, only to fall back into the same vicious cycle in the near future.

The rather complex IT environment in most organizations today is normally considered the culprit to effectively tackle performance issues. The argument made here is that performance has to be designed into the final solution. This approach requires shifting the emphasis away from the installation and setup phase to the planning and design stages. It is paramount that organizations not only understand the expected workload behavior, but act upon accordingly by conducting feasibility and design studies prior to spending thousand of dollars on a solution that in a best case scenario, may not be optimal, and in a worst case scenario, just dose not work.

Performance Design Considerations

Application performance issues have an immediate impact on customer satisfaction and an organization's bottom line. It is not uncommon that while a performance issue surfaces, organizations start adding more (expensive) hardware into the operation mix, without fully understanding where the problem really is. Hence, working on the symptoms and not actually tackling the problem may provide an organization with some relieve in the short run, but intensifies the issues in the long run, as even more hardware has to be troubleshooted and analyzed. In addition to hardware costs, the IT personnel costs associated with unplanned performance tuning exercises can be excruciating. IT managers may be forced to commit hundreds of man-hours to solve even simpler performance problems. As in some circumstances, the actual source of the problem may not be easily identified, IT personnel may spend hours or days analyzing and tuning the wrong subsystem. To make matters worse, some performance tuning exercises may require crossing over into the domains of security, reliability, or availability. Without initial proper planning, fire-fighting scenarios such as these may result into additional work for an organization's security or high-availability (HA) personnel as well.

To reiterate, the proper approach to managing systems performance is to design performance into a solution [4]. If a system is already in production, the recommendation made is to conduct an in-depth performance study that includes the applications, the operating system, and the hardware subsystems, respectively. It is paramount to understand not only the actual workload behavior, but also the interaction among the applications, the operating system, and the hardware. Establishing a sound performance baseline allows an organization to proactively manage performance while the workload changes, and to conduct a capacity study based on facts and not on fiction. Treading performance related issues early on in an IT project allows getting away from the hidden cost scenarios, and is exponentially cheaper than to perform the tuning as an add-on feature after a problem surfaced. Fortuitous Technologies offers application, database, operating system, and hardware design, feasibility, performance tuning, and capacity planning services that are vendor independent, and only focus on the actual environment that a corporation has (or will have) in production.

Performance Modeling

Building efficient applications as hierarchical compositions of cooperating components (modules) depends significantly on having a thorough knowledge of both, component performance, as well as component interaction. Hence, to make effective decisions concerning configuration, deployment, and interconnection, it is important to develop a Performance Engineering (PE) methodology that complements the traditional application development processes. Ideally, performance techniques such as measurement, analysis, and modeling, which extend the programming and execution environment to be both, performance observable and performance aware, should support the methodology. However, the diversity of functionality and the complexity of the implementations (such as different programming languages, hardware platforms, and thread parallelism modes) challenge the area of performance technology to offer more sound solutions.

The discipline of Software Engineering (SE) incorporates the procedures, methods, and tools that control the software development process [3],[4]. SE provides the foundation for building high quality software products in an efficient and effective manner. There are many dimensions to software quality, including availability, maintainability, scalability, functionality, flexibility, security, and performance. Many of the SE methodologies in use today only focus on ensuring that the software product meets functional requirements, while being developed within a certain time-frame and financial budget. In today's market place, performance requirements are increasingly difficult to manage, while at the same time, are getting more and more exposed. The deployment of complex, multi-tier, client-server based software systems causes a pure analytical modeling based performance analyses approach to become much more complex (while still very valuable though), resulting into performance models that require a much more in-depth experience in mathematics and queuing theory. Just as the nature of the software and computer systems has evolved, so has the user community. Most enterprises no longer design, develop, and deploy systems for their own internal use only, as today's systems are primarily intended for direct customer contact. The evolution of the Internet (particularly the area of E-commerce) has placed a much higher emphasis on systems availability, maintainability, and scalability (with a main focus on actual systems performance).

This article outlines a methodology that *enables systems performance engineering.* The underlying focus is on avoiding the case where performance issues are being identified in either the system test phase, in quality assurance, or even in the initial deployment phase. Mitigating any potential performance risks (early on in the systems life cycle), determining and evaluating systems scalability (based on additional physical and logical resources that are made available), as well as evaluating the aspects of systems support, are the key components that directly contribute and impact the methodology. The argument being made is that in order to evaluate *end-to-end performance in a multi-tier environment,* the combination of an analytical and a Petri-Net based (simulation) modeling approach is applicable, as it enables analyzing and evaluating the *dynamics* of an entire infrastructure. This includes any potential outside influences, such as other applications that compete for the shared (hardware and or software) resources. Similar to data modeling, prototyping, or use-case studies conducted by the software design and development teams, Petri-Net based simulation modeling is focused on elaborating, evaluating, and analyzing systems performance under a variety of circumstances. Simulation modeling involves developing, calibrating, verifying, validating, and utilizing a model of an entire system to analyze, evaluate, and estimate key performance metrics such as response time, throughput, and resource utilization. The actual model is derived from either Sequence Diagrams (SD) or Use Case Maps (UCM) that are provided by the design team, and incorporates the hardware and software infrastructure as determined by the systems architects.

Where to Start

In a commercial environment, a *business process* is the driving factor that triggers the actual need for a system. As a user performs a certain task on the system, the application is called upon to basically retrieve data, to perform calculations or comparisons, and to update information. Essential to the performance engineering process is an estimate of *the volume of work* that has to be performed. The *volume of work* is being considered as one of the input parameters into either the analytical or the simulation model. To reiterate, a user application supports the execution of a business process. When being invoked, an application (either through library or system calls) utilizes actual physical and logical resources. Some of the key physical resources are the CPU, memory, I/O, and network related components, whereas some of the logical resources can be identified as the memory tables, the file system block sizes, or the network packet sizes. The called upon resources have to be identified and quantified, as they represent additional input parameters into the model. In practice, these resources are either determined through an educated guessing process, are being extracted from a similar system through an empirical analysis, or are derived from an 'instrumented' prototype that mimics the actual system. As an example, by utilizing tools such as ARM, in conjunction with a prototype, the application can report detailed response time measurements for each *individual business function component*, as well as for the entire transaction [8]. As an example, based on the collected data, it is feasible to separate the think time from the actual system processing time, and to determine which application functionality contributes the most to the overall response time or resource utilization.

Methodology to Conduct End-to-End Performance Analysis

Retrofitting performance improvements into an existing product is a daunting and expensive task, and may delay the deploying of the system. The following section outlines a very pragmatic, *divide-and-conquer* based approach, which consists of several cascading steps that can be transformed into a comprehensive systems performance analysis. The methodology utilizes studies conducted by Smith, Jain, Siddiqui et al. as a blueprint (see references). In a nutshell, the overall system is basically divided up into parts that correspond to system responsibilities that are identified as having a certain performance budget. Utilizing the performance budgets (the budgets are either being guessed or determined through an empirical analysis), a system's overall performance can be estimated and potential design changes can be analyzed dynamically. To reiterate, the analytical or simulation models can not only be used to predict overall response time, but also to define and evaluate certain performance goals. In other words, feasible performance budgets can be determined and quantified to meet the overall performance goals, resulting into a process that can be described as supporting an incremental change in performance analysis.

Based on the complexity of the system and the question to be answered, either the analytical or the simulation model is the key to understanding the individual performance budgets, and to meet the overall performance goal. Once the model is developed, the analysis can be conducted either by utilizing a *forward* or a *reverse direction* based analysis approach. In a *forward direction* based analysis, the logical flow starts with the individual performance budgets and ends up with an overall quantification of the entire system, ergo can be used to conduct a feasibility analysis in regards to the system's requirements. As already discussed, the initial performance budgets might have to be determined either based on experience (normally incorporating a *reserve* for contingencies), or by utilizing a prototype-based approach. *A reverse direction* based study incorporates an analysis that starts with the overall performance goal that is being decomposed into individual performance budgets (on a per operation level). The reverse path based approach basically generates (again, on a per-operation based level) the *has-to-be-achieved* individual performance budgets, and might serve as a tool to identify infeasible performance goals.

Step 1: Design Specification

The design specification captures the system behavior as a set of scenarios (at a certain level of abstraction), outlining the invoked software subsystems, operations and responsibilities on a per business function level. Sequence Diagrams (SD) or Use Case Maps (UCM) provide the flexibility and detail necessary to develop the model, and to conduct sensitivity and capacity studies [1],[2].

Step 2: Performance (Demand) Budgets

It is imperative to not only identify the performance goals prior to any modeling activities, but also to have a very clear picture of what performance questions are supposed to be answered in the study. This is crucial as the performance goals *drive the level of (modeling) detail necessary* to answer the performance questions. The individual performance budgets are actual values that describe the resource demand of the operations and responsibilities as identified in the SD or the UCM. As an example, the units to be determined could be in CPU-seconds, operation counts, packet sizes, or Mbytes moved through the networking and/or the I/O subsystem. To reiterate, the initial budgets have to be either assumed or guessed based on experience, derived from a similar system, measured utilizing existing components, or determined based on a empirical analysis conducted by using a prototype. Further, it is imperative to identify certain *workload profiles* that identify the set of *operation mixes* (as being anticipated in real world scenarios).

Step 3: Identifying the Hardware, Software, and Communication Infrastructure

The application specifications do not completely define an entire system per se. In most performance studies that operate in a multi-tier environment, it is necessary to obtain the hardware layout, the operating system specifications, as well as the incorporated network and middle-ware infrastructure from the architecture team [7]. All these elements have to be determined prior to developing the model (this process might be assumption based as well).

Step 4: Developing the (Stochastic Simulation) Model

While conducting a performance analysis, analysts normally utilize a combination of analytical model, simulation model, and empirical analysis based techniques. An analytical model simulates the behavior of a system, is build through equations, and the actual performance is derived mathematically. With an analytical model, it is normally necessary to construct a number of parameterized functions that approximate the workload characteristics of the system components [4]. In other words, an analytical model provides *average* and *standard deviation* types of statistics, as the actual workload distribution is *normally* ignored. A number of simplifying assumptions has to be made to trace the model. How these assumptions reflect the real world behavior and the extent to which they can be formulated as mathematical equations basically determines the accuracy and usefulness of this approach. Analytical models are generally cheaper and faster to build than simulation models, and can easily be tailored to analyze and predict (after calibrating the model) a wide variety of performance-related aspects of a system.

Simulation models on the other hand consist of a suite of modules or programs that are designed to capture the characteristics of a system under real world conditions. The basic idea is to model the entire system and to simulate its dynamic behavior by taking the actual workload distribution into account. More specifically, each event (or state transition) in a computing environment is being considered, analyzed, and modeled. Simulation models are normally rather complex, and hence more expensive to build than an analytical model, but may provide a higher degree of accuracy (and are extensively being used to conduct sensitivity studies) [4].

An empirical analysis on the other hand involves executing an application or benchmark program on an *existing system* and to measure actual performance [4]. This approach provides the most accurate performance data of the three discussed techniques, but it only analyzes one specific workload (the one that is being executed with a specific set of parameter values) and normally can not be used to conduct a sensitivity analysis per se. In some circumstances, this approach can be very time intensive (and expensive), as the test environment either has to be made available, or has to be built from scratch. To re-emphasize, most performance studies consist of a mixture of the three approaches discussed in this article. The proper approach (that is applicable to conduct the analysis) is chosen based on *the performance goals and the to-be-answered performance questions.*

Commercial simulation modeling tools, such as the HyPerformix Infrastructure Optimizer (IO), represent actual state-event systems where a task can be analyzed as it flows through an entire system, while *visiting* different software and hardware components

[9]. On the other hand, deterministic stochastic Petri-net (DSPN) solutions (some DSPN packages are available as freeware) are utilized to facilitate and formulate the high-level modeling abstractions of discrete-event systems that consist of exponential and deterministic subtasks. The data collected in steps 1, 2 and 3 of the outlined methodology serves as the blueprint to develop and calibrate the model. If the individual performance budgets were obtained by conducting an empirical analysis, the final model can be verified and validated against the actually measured systems performance (to ensure that the model reflects reality, and can be used to conduct a comprehensive sensitivity or capacity study). If the model cannot be validated at this stage of the system life cycle, the model can be used (as an example) in the design phase to evaluate different design alternatives. Further, it is feasible to analyze and quantify the impact that an infrastructure change has on systems performance, an approach that might require normalizing the performance data, as the analysis is now focused on relative and not on actual performance.

Step 5: Analysis and Recommendations

Running an actual simulation (either in a homogeneous or heterogeneous environment) allows comparing the obtained (simulation based) results to the actual performance requirements. An artifact of running a simulation is to utilize the performance results to verify that *if the performance budgets are being met*, overall systems performance is adequate. Another benefit is the potential of adjusting the capacity of certain physical (such as the CPU speed) and logical (such as the number of concurrent worker threads) resources, so that given the overall performance budget, the performance goals might either be met or more closely be approached [5],[6]. In general, actual recommendations on how to improve performance (by for example either altering the design or adjusting hardware or software components) are *result dependent*. In most circumstances, changes are required if overall performance does not meet the goals. A best practice approach is to change one component (in the model) at a time, and to rerun the simulation after the change has been implemented to clearly understand, quantify, and document the progress.

Summary

A modeling based approach (normally in conjunction with other tools and techniques) is applicable throughout the system life cycle. In the design phase, evaluating overall performance, analyzing and quantifying different design alternatives and/or different hardware configurations is imperative to mitigate the risk of encountering (expensive) performance deficiencies later on in the project. In most cases, in the development phase (where more performance related data becomes available), the model can be re-calibrated and additional sensitivity and capacity studies can be conducted. This evolutionary process generally leads to comprehensive test scenarios that can be simulated in the (stress) test phase. The outlined methodology enables a comprehensive performance analysis and documentation process that can further be used as a communication tool among the involved design, development, and test teams. The process represents the common denominator for all the involved parties, and can be considered as the tool that drives most of the technical discussions. A sequel to this article will discuss an actual 3-tier architecture and elaborate on the combination of analytical and simulation models that were being used to conduct the PE project.

References

1.   Buhr, R., "Use Case Maps for Object Oriented Systems", Prentice-Hall, 1995

2.   Franks, G., Majumdar, S., "Performance Analysis of Distributed Server Systems", 6th International Conference on Software Quality, Ottawa, Canada, 1996

3.   Hennessy, J., Patterson, D., "Computer Architecture, a Quantitative Approach", Third Edition, Morgan Kaufmann, 2002.

4.   Jain, R., "The Art of Computer System Performance Analysis", John Wiley, 1991

5.   Koenigs, A. "Industrial Strength Parallel Computing", Morgan Kaufmann, San Francisco, 2000

6.   Siddiqui, K., "Time Performance Budgeting of Software Design", Masters Thesis, Carleton University, Ottawa, Canada, 2001

7.   Pfister, G. F., "In Search of Clusters", Second Edition, Prentice Hall PTR, NY, 1998.

8.   ARM for JAVA http://regions.cmg.org/regions/cmgarmw/CMG00_paper_final.pdf

9.   Infrastructure Optimizer (HyPerformix) http://www.hyperformix.com

Chapter 6 - Reliability Engineering - Business Aspects, Concepts, and Tools

Introduction

An emerging consensus in the systems performance community is that the traditional performance centric focus has become misdirected, and that issues such as reliability, availability, and scalability have emerged as being as important as peak systems performance. The basic term *availability* carries many potential connotations. Traditionally, availability has been defined as a binary metric that basically describes whether a system is up or down. A common extension of this definition is to compute the percentage of time that the system is on average available. *Reliability* on the other hand can be expressed as the probability that a failure situation will not emerge over a certain period of time in the future. The argument made is that reliability and availability are closely related terms, but that they are not interchangeable entities per se, as they represent different expressions revolving around the same issue. While both dimensions are closely related to the overall stability of a system (or an application component), reliability focuses on failure rate based statistics whereas availability represents the measure of time a system or application component is operational. The goal of this primer was to briefly elaborate on the similarities and differences among reliability and availability, and to introduce some of the tools, concepts, and business implications that surround reliability engineering.

Reliability Engineering Concepts

Reliability is the probability of any hardware or software component to function without failure when operated correctly for a given time interval under stated conditions. Hardware and software component failures cost money and cause unreliability issues and concerns. The business focus on reliability revolves around controlling the failure rate to reduce overall costs and to improve operations by enhancing the overall business performance by utilizing affordable levels of reliability [1],[3].

An interesting artifact of any reliability analysis is the reference to reliability, but actually measuring or quantifying failure rates. A failure situation demonstrates the evidence of a lack of reliability in an infrastructure. Reliability problems are expressed as failures, and failures cost money in any economic enterprise. In most circumstances, failures result into a form of a *downtime scenario*. The argument made is that the process of the *definition of failure* that leads to an increased need for reliability improvements is paramount. Failure situations normally galvanize organizations to take action. The fact of the matter is that in most circumstances, the actual funding for reliability improvements comes from the cost of unreliability. At the center of any reliability improvement study has to be the need to find affordable solutions. Successful reliability engineering work can be described as the perpetual quest for affordable improvements that result in increased profits by solving the most important reliability problems [8]. Effective reliability engineering can not be described as the *quest for perfection*, but rather the search for effective business solutions to resolve the issues that cause the majority of the failure situations.

In most circumstances however, raw reliability numbers do not provide the motivation for actual business improvements. The raw reliability numbers have to be converted into monetary values that express the cost of encountering *unreliability*. Annualizing any losses by means of the cost of unreliability immediately identifies the amount of money that should be available to rectify reliability issues [2]. As with systems performance, purchasing more hardware components without conducting an in-depth analysis of the infrastructure results into working on the symptoms without resolving the actual problem, and has to be considered as being counterproductive in the long run [9]. Reliability requirements fluctuate based on the competitive conditions of the market place. Ergo, reliability values are not immutable as they change along with the business conditions.

The ramification is that the different business conditions require the use of different reliability engineering tools for resolving the business problems [4]. Reliability engineering tools such as Failure Reporting and Corrective Action Systems (FRACAS), design reviews, decision trees, Failure Mode and Effects Analysis (FMEA), Fault Tree Analysis (FTA), or Reliability Qualification Tests (RQT) are available to support the effort. The issue is that no company can afford too little or too much reliability, which transforms into another exercise in compromises in regards to the overall systems stability scenario. The cost of unreliability has to be engineered and controlled, which implies that the discussed reliability tools have to be utilized in a cost-effective manner.

Failure Mode and Effects Analysis (FMEA)

The FMEA technique is considered as representing a pervasive reliability engineering methodology that can be applied in a vast variety of areas, focusing on hardware as well as software components, respectively. The intention of FMEA is to identify potential failure modes of any system components, evaluate the impact on the system behavior, and to propose appropriate countermeasures to suppress these effects. To emphasize, the focus has to be on failure prevention and not on failure detection per se. The FMEA technique is well established at a system and hardware component level where the potential failure modes are usually known and can easily be quantified. In other words, FMEA represents a systematic way of identifying any potential failure modes of a system or function, and allows evaluating the effects of the failure modes on any (potential) higher level of abstraction [5],[6].

The objective is to determine the cause for the failure modes and what could be done to eliminate or at least economize on the probability of failure. FMEA is best described as a bottom-up based methodology where the system under scrutiny is hierarchically divided into sub-components. The decomposition has to be conducted in such a way that the failure modes of the components at the bottom level can be identified. The failure effects of the lower level components constitute to the failure modes of the upper level components. After identifying the decomposition approach, the next step is to define the failure mode, the failure effects, as well as the failure cause of the actual component (see Figure 6-1).

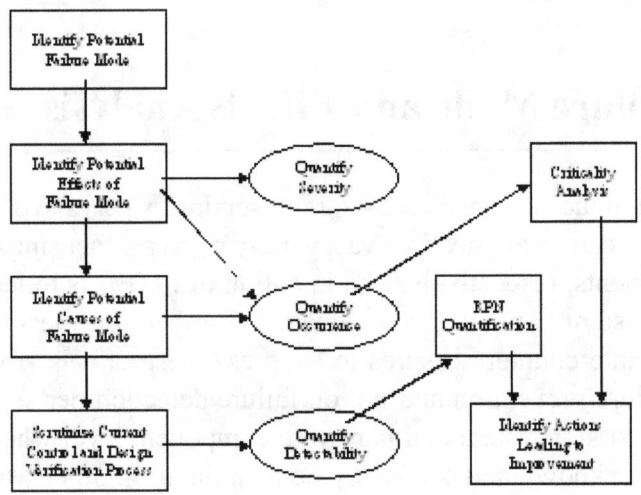

Figure 6-1: FMEA Roadmap

For each component, the severity, the occurrence, and in some cases the detection variable has to be quantified. The severity variable represents a rating that corresponds to the seriousness of an effect of a potential failure mode. The occurrence variable depicts a rating that corresponds to the rate at which a first level cause and its resultant failure mode will occur over a certain life span. The detection variable discusses a rating that corresponds to the likelihood that the detection methods or the current control infrastructure will detect the potential failure mode over a certain time span. All three variables are normally expressed on a scale from 1 to 10. In most cases, hardware manufacturers provide the analyst with detailed information on the failure modes and frequencies of their occurrence. The actual interpretation of an FMEA analysis normally revolves either around the Risk Priority Number (RPN) method or focuses on an actual Criticality Analysis [7]. The RPN identifies the greatest areas of concern by comprising the assessment of the severity, the occurrence, and the detection ratings, respectively. In other words, the RPN represents the product of the three variables.

The term Criticality Analysis (CA) on the other hand describes another quantitative extension to the FMEA technique that is only based on the severity of the failure effects and the frequency of the failure occurrence. The CA analysis is considered as being more proactive than the RPN method, as an RPN based approach assigns an equal weight to the detection variable. The argument made is that before an organization should allocate resources to improve the detection mechanism, all opportunities for reducing the occurrence and minimizing the effects of the failure modes should be explored. The recommendation is that a comprehensive analysis should incorporate a combination of the severity level, the CA, and the RPN to decide when corrective actions have to be taken. The thesis made is that the severity level and the CA analysis should always be consulted while conducting an FMEA study. The following experiment (Table 6-1) elaborates on the different conclusions that might be drawn if an analysis is solely based on the (popular) RPN method:

Table 6-1: RPN Analysis

Failure Mode	Severity	Occurrence	Detection	RPN
FM1	4	4	10	160
FM2	5	9	2	90
FM3	9	3	1	27

In this particular scenario, FM1 represents the failure mode with the highest RPN. Conducting a CA study focusing on the severity and occurrence variables leads to an area chart that divides the spectrum of the two variables into three sections that represent the high, the medium, and the low priority failure modes (see Figure 2). Based on the area chart, the failure modes FM2 and FM3 represent high priority failure modes, whereas the failure mode with the highest RPN only represents a medium priority failure mode. Quantifying the detection rate is in many circumstances rather ambiguous, ergo the recommendation to always evaluate the RPN in conjunction with a CA study. The severity in itself bears a lot of merit and should always be scrutinized first. A severity of 8, 9, or 10 (10 representing a potentially hazardous failure) should automatically result into launching a *corrective action* process. The strategy for addressing the actual failure modes should follow the following layout:

1. Eliminate the occurrence

2. Reduce the severity

3. Reduce the occurrence

4. Improve the detection

5. Provide a means of detection

On the software side, the failure modes are generally unknown, as a lot of software modules do not fail in the same way as hardware components. In most circumstances, software components deliver incorrect results and depend on the dynamic behavior of the application workload itself. When considering FMEA for a software application (SWFMEA), the utmost purpose of the analysis usually revolves around identifying the software faults that in some circumstances could jeopardize the proper functionality of the system [6]. It has to be emphasized that compared to hardware components, software modules do not wear out in a physical sense, they deteriorate. The deterioration is not a function of time but a side effect of changes (a function of usage) made in the maintenance phase to correct defects, to adjust the application to changing requirements, or to improve performance.

Further, SWFMEA should not be considered as a replacement for traditional software reliability methods. SWFMEA is intended to be a systematic thinking method, or more specifically a means of anticipating issues and improving the validation process. Never less, FMEA can be utilized in all phases of the system life cycle from the requirement specification to the design, implementation, operation, and maintenance phases, respectively [7]. The largest return on investment can be found in the early phases of the design, where FMEA (DFMEA) can be used to isolate problem areas in the systems structure and thus avoid expensive design changes later on in the life cycle.

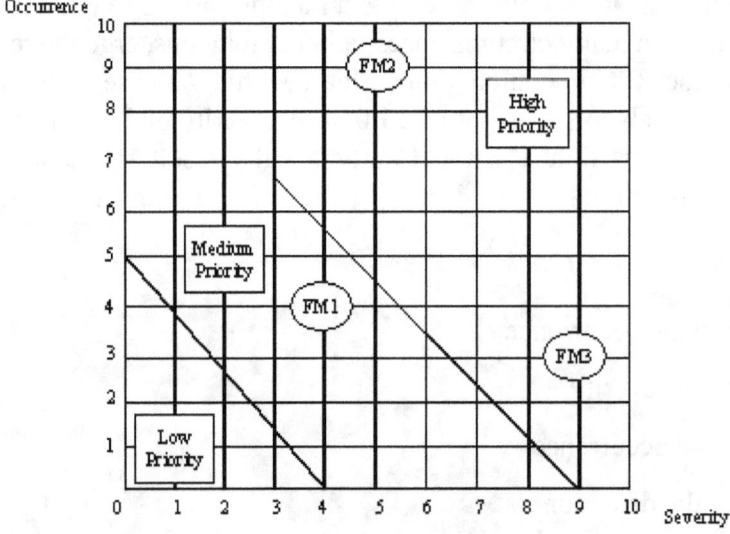

Figure 6-2: Area Chart

To support FMEA in a software environment, the recommendation is to utilize additional techniques such as a Fault Tree Analysis (FTA). As a fault tree based approach is considered a static technique that does not reach all the dynamic aspects of a software subsystem, the FTA technique in itself has to be combined with a Petri Net or a Dynamic Flow Graph analysis, respectively. As already elaborated, software component failure modes are normally unknown as if a failure mode would be known it would hopefully be corrected. Therefore, the definition of failure modes is the biggest challenge while applying FMEA to software components. The analysis has to be based on existing knowledge surrounding the software components and requires postulating the relevant failure modes.

Summary

This chapter outlined the importance of understanding the interrelationship between availability and reliability while conducting an analysis either on a systems component or an application task level. Reliability is paramount in modern computer systems, in some circumstances even at the expense of systems performance. A slower but reliable system might be acceptable whereas any failure situation or data loss issues might have a catastrophic impact on the user community. Any downtime could potentially be equally unacceptable, which leads to the importance of high systems availability. Further, this report outlined that *availability* and *reliability* are not interchangeable terms, as a system might reveal a high availability but at the same time discloses a low reliability behavior (or vice versa). As an example, a network router is a physical device that does not store any state data. Hence it can be considered as one of the few physical resources where a data loss is acceptable as long as high availability standards are maintained. Every reliability and availability analysis is *environment specific* and has to be conducted by taking the entire computing infrastructure into consideration. Analyzing and scrutinize the impact that any potential changes will have on systems performance and systems maintenance is paramount. Dependability, scalability, as well as maintainability components impact the overall systems stability. Only a high ranking in all three dimensions will result into an overall useful, trustworthy, and effective computing environment.

References

1.   Dellin, T., "*Yield and Reliability*", Sandia National Laboratories, 1998

2.   Dugan, J., "*On Measurement and Modeling of Computer Systems Dependability*", IEEE Transactions on Reliability, Vol. 39, Oct. 1990.

3.   Edmiston, P., Peng, J., "*Reliability and Availability of Networked Client-Server Systems*, CMG, 1993

4.   Johnson, M., Malek, M., "*Survey of Software Tools for Evaluating Reliability, Availability, and Serviceability,*" ACM Computing Vol. 20, Dec. 1988.

5.   Palady, P., "*FMEA – Author's Edition*", 2nd Edition, 1997

6.   Pentti, H., Atte, H., "*Failure Mode and Effects Analysis of Software Based Automation Systems*", VTT, 2002

7.   Price., K., "*Failure Mode & Effects Analysis in Software Development*", SAE Technical Paper, 1998

8.   Sahner R., Trivedi, K., "*Reliability Modeling*" IEEE Transactions on Reliability, June 1987.

9.   BU, "*Effective Processing Time Modeling*", Boston University, 2002

Chapter 7 - Maintenance Systems

Introduction

In this chapter, maintenance activities are discussed from a systemic point of view. Maintenance is considered from the selected viewpoint as a control system for controlling the reliability of machines in a process environment. While this chapter branches out a bit into the industrial world, it has to be pointed out that the actual control process takes place through communication of information. Hence, maintenance can also be considered as an information processing system. Therefore, the viewpoint presented in this chapter also supports the development of maintenance information systems.

Maintenance Conditions

The term maintenance includes various actions and tasks that aim to increase or to retain the reliability of the machines. A term often presented is *maintenance policy*, which refers to the categories of the maintenance actions applied. Depending on the industry and the applied maintenance paradigm the terms of the categories vary. Such terms include condition-based maintenance, failure-based maintenance, preventive maintenance, predictive maintenance, reactive maintenance and corrective maintenance Principally all the categories refer to the timing or methodology of the maintenance activity.

The main categorization is maintenance activities that happen before and after a failure. Therefore, the term's *proactive maintenance* and *reactive maintenance* are used [3]. Proactive and reactive maintenance may be *planned* or *unplanned*. This means that the work procedures of the maintenance action and its required resources are either planned or unplanned before the need for the maintenance action. A maintenance action for a failure that has never before occurred is difficult to plan beforehand. Therefore, reactive maintenance is often thought as a synonym for unplanned maintenance. However, planning for reactive maintenance can be done if the required maintenance procedures are known.

For example, the replacement procedures and resource requirements of a disk failure can be planned even if the maintenance action is reactive. Proactive maintenance action can be *preventive* or *predictive*. Preventive maintenance tries to prevent a failure before its occurrence with such activities as lubricating, cleaning or changing a wearing component. Predictive maintenance, also know as *condition-based maintenance*, tries to detect the machine condition automatically or manually, for executing the maintenance action based on the actual condition of the machine. *Scheduled maintenance* is a proactive maintenance action that has been scheduled beforehand according to a plan. Proactive maintenance can be scheduled, but reactive maintenance can never be scheduled in advance [5],[6].

Maintenance Processes

As an activity, maintenance can be described as a business process. The term is a bit fuzzy and overloaded. The idea of a business process concept is that there are several sequential activities that form an information processing chain. A business process can be defined as *a collection of interrelated work tasks, initiated in response to an event, that achieves a specific result for the customer of the process. This* definition emphasizes that the process instance is triggered by an event, and consists of work tasks to satisfy the customer needs. In some cases the information systems and business processes cannot be separated. The information system implements a business process and enables the process workflow. Therefore, it is important to understand the maintenance process in order to model the effects of information systems [1].

Detailed description of a maintenance process is difficult. The implementation of the process workflow depends on the applied industry and company. The model is general and should be suitable for describing most maintenance processes. Its informative value is not very high, but it should be accurate enough to provide an understanding of the activities in maintenance systems. The triggering events for maintenance processes are (1) reactive failure event, usually in form of a failure report or work request, (2) condition-based maintenance event, from inspections or automatic condition monitoring, (3) preventive maintenance event, from preventive maintenance program, and (4) backlog event, from a work queue that should have already been done. The previous initiating events indicate that there is a queue of work to be done. This queue is filled with work orders arising from failures. The maintenance staff that maintains the systems processes the work orders. The failures may be predicted by inspecting the systems or by using automatic condition monitoring. Manual inspection is a periodic activity triggered by a watchdog subsystem that monitors the time or usage of the machine, thus creating a maintenance work order that is placed in the queue. Preventive maintenance is similar to inspections: a time or usage monitoring system triggers the maintenance action, and the order is placed in the queue. Queuing theory-based models can be used to present the maintenance resource allocation.

Depending on the viewpoint, the customer of the maintenance process is either the production process owner or the production system owner. The production process requires functional systems, and hence the quality and efficiency of the maintenance process directly affect the production process. On the other hand, the system owner has invested money in the machines and expects long-term profitability from the investment. The production process owner and system owner are not necessarily the same organization. There are situations where a system is leased from a leasing company to an institution. The main activities in maintenance are planning, scheduling and execution [2]. Planning consists of planning the actual work activities and the resource needs, such as tools, materials and work skills for the maintenance task.

Scheduling consists of arranging the maintenance tasks in the right order and time concerning the production plan and resource availability. Execution of the maintenance task consists of such activities as installation, inspection, modification, restoration and repair. In addition to these there are some supporting activities such as recording failures, work requests, maintenance execution reports, system configuration changes and administration of reporting, budgeting, engineering, and inventory control.

The reactive maintenance process begins with a failure or possible failure identification. The failure is then diagnosed. Diagnosing is an activity that may require several participants from specialists to production personnel. After the failure is diagnosed, repair is planned and parts are ordered. After that, the repair is scheduled, and the work is ordered. When the parts are available, the machine is repaired according to the schedule. The process flow diagram indicates that the notification, diagnostics, planning and dispatching time as well as the repair time itself affect the throughput, or cycle time of reactive maintenance. Therefore, failure notification, diagnostics, planning, scheduling, or work order dispatching should be more efficient to increase the efficiency of the process. Keeping a stock of parts available for maintenance can reduce logistics delay.

The proactive maintenance process flow does not include the diagnostics stage. In practice, this is not always true. When using condition monitoring, there may be signs of future failures, which makes it possible to predict a failure. The symptoms may be so clear that there is no need for diagnostics, but if the symptoms are unknown (or contradictory), there may be a similar diagnostics stage as in reactive maintenance. Failure prediction marks the beginning of a process, as well as the preventive event that is created according to machine operating time or other usage measurement. If the process is well designed and pre-planned, the waiting time from the event to the beginning of maintenance execution should be much shorter than in the reactive process [4]. Also, the parts can be ordered *before* the failure occurs so that they are ready for use when needed. The process flows indicate that proactive maintenance is quicker and more easily standardizable than the reactive process. However, the contents of the process planning and execution stages of proactive maintenance depend on the failure type. Furthermore, the cost of failures and the maintenance, rather than the efficiency of the processes alone define the feasibility of proactive and reactive maintenance.

Business Aspects

Proactive maintenance can be seen as a method to convert variable costs of failures to fixed costs of maintenance. Maintenance is expense to the owner of the systems, but also a business opportunity to the spare parts and maintenance service providers. The maintenance costs and revenues are the main drivers for controlling the reliability of machines and the efficiency of maintenance processes.

The costs can be divided into direct and indirect costs. Direct costs are related to the efficiency of the maintenance processes and they are easier to calculate than indirect costs. Indirect costs are related to the effectiveness of the maintenance process to reliable production. Also, too high production capacity, or over-maintaining, as well as the supporting activities, such as production personnel support for the maintenance personnel, can be calculated as indirect costs. Maintenance costs are often allocated to the maintenance department. If maintenance is looked at as a revenue-generating business, the main focus is on the maintenance contracts, which are based on the work time and materials consumed or on the parts sales, repairs and refurbishing [2]. The services, such as training or support, are a complementary source of revenues. A maintenance contract usually covers the normal work and materials and guarantees a specific service level with a fixed yearly price. Therefore, the maintenance service provider benefits from enhancing the maintenance processes.

Maintenance Systems Control

Feed-forward control with preventive maintenance assumes that after some usage the risk for system failures is high and the system should be therefore maintained. However, the actual effectiveness of the maintenance systems can be measured only with the help of the occurred failures. Paradoxically, not many failures can be observed in an effective maintenance system. Consequently, the maintenance system efficiency becomes known only in the long run, making quick control difficult and slow control too slow. Additionally, the uncertainty in the failure and maintenance system dynamics, and the possible variances in repeatability of the maintenance actions make the effect of control actions vary and thus reduces reliability. Often, the effects of preventive maintenance can be seen several years after that maintenance action.

Long delays of failure processes make failure feed-back-based adjustments to the preventive maintenance program uncertain. Unexpected number of failures causes challenges to maintain the proactive maintenance program [6]. Fire-fighting breakdowns reduce the possibility to do condition-based and preventive maintenance. This may cause more failures later. Insufficient worker resources make the maintenance systems respond more slowly to the needs to increase the proportion of proactive maintenance. Also, correct selection of maintenance system efficiency measurement metrics is critical. If not using total cost of maintenance and failures as the controlled variable the control may become irrational and favors some maintenance policies more than others. In summary, slow system dynamics make optimal maintenance system control very difficult.

Effect of Condition Monitoring on Maintenance Systems

Observability defines the key relationship between a machine and a maintenance system. Without observations it is impossible to say anything about reliability, repeatability, efficiency or controllability. Therefore, in addition to human perceptions, condition monitoring is the only way to measure how a maintenance system performs. Condition-based and preventive maintenance is not mutually exclusive maintenance policies. Compared to preventive maintenance only, condition-based maintenance may yield much more efficient maintenance systems. However, condition monitoring is not likely to be fully accurate or it is too slow compared to all the failure types. Thus, condition-based maintenance should not always be considered as a replacing, but a complementing policy to preventive maintenance. Mixing preventive maintenance and condition-based maintenance may yield the most optimal results. More speedy reaction to a possible failure increases the proportion of the failures that a maintenance system can prevent. Therefore, a computerized maintenance management system and a condition monitoring system may support each other [1]. However, in reality, a formal maintenance process workflow may be bypassed in order to execute the condition-based maintenance action in time. Repairing in a hurry is quite likely more error-prone than well-planned proactive maintenance.

Condition-based maintenance reduces failures and increases the proportion of proactive maintenance. In theory, this would lead consequently to more sufficient worker resources and therefore would also increase the controllability of the maintenance system. The research supported the other studies about the reduction of supply chain variability if sharing consumption information by using condition monitoring. This represents a novel and practical idea of linking the component replacement information directly from the machines to the manufacturer-end of the supply chain. Compared to the other results of the research, this may turn out as the most valuable short-term application area of the research. In summary, condition monitoring can be seen as a method for increasing system observability and therefore an enabler for more effective maintenance systems. However, the effect of condition monitoring depends on the accuracy of the monitoring and the failure diagnosis, and is also affected by the failure patterns, the repeatability of maintenance actions and the delay to arrange the maintenance actions. In spare parts supply chains, remote condition monitoring can be used to stabilize the supply chain variability and to reduce the supply chain sensitivity to random noise and sudden changes in the consumption.

Summary

The viewpoint of this research was that of maintenance systems and system control. The effect of condition monitoring on the maintenance systems was studied by reviewing maintenance and systems literature, as well as by using conceptual and mathematical models. Most of the research papers and literature related to this research have been written from the reliability point of view. That is, the objective has been in modeling and improvement of machine or production line reliability. Although it is necessary to understand the use of reliability engineering techniques in order to control the reliability of machines, it is at least equally important to understand the maintenance systems and their control to efficiently reach and maintain the required reliability.

Preventive maintenance is feed-forward control and reactive maintenance is feed-back control. Condition-based maintenance represents neither pure feed-forward nor pure feed-back control. If the preventive maintenance schedule is changed according to the occurred failures, the maintenance system can be considered an adaptive system with a high-level feed-back control. Information systems and automatic condition monitoring cannot be applied efficiently if these fundamental control activities and the information flows of the maintenance systems are not understood.

References

1.   Endrenyi, J. (2001) The present status of maintenance strategies and the impact of maintenance on reliability. IEEE Transactions on Power Systems, Vol. 16, Issue 4, pp. 638-646.

2.   File, T. (1991) Cost effective maintenance: design and implementation. Oxford, UK, Butterworth-Heinemann Ltd.

3.   IEC 61025 (1990) Fault tree analysis (FTA). International Electrotechnical Commission.

4.   Kerr, R. (1991) Knowledge-based manufacturing management: Applications of artificial intelligence to the effective management of manufacturing companies. Singapore, Addison-Wesley Publishing Company Inc.

5.   Lee J. (2001) A framework for Web-enabled e-maintenance systems. Proceedings of EcoDesign 2001: Second International Symposium on 2001, pp. 450-459.

6.   Wolovich, W. (2000) Controllability and observability. In: Levine, W. (ed.) (2000) Control system fundamentals. Boca Raton, FL, USA, CRC Press LLC, pp. 121-130.

Chapter 8 - Using Statistical Data to Analyze Reliability & to Schedule Maintenance

Introduction

Maintenance scheduling or Reliability studies do not have to be based solely on an expert opinion. By carefully recording failure data, or using failure data from manufacturers, maintenance schedules and reliability studies can be economically optimized by utilizing statistical methods. The preventive maintenance discussed in Chapter 7 is further illustrated in this chapter.

Preventive maintenance may be considered the de-facto method; maintenance is performed to prevent failures that are due to wear. Examples are changing hoses, changing belts, or routine cleaning activities. Inspections are used to reduce the impact of failures that are not catastrophic. Considering the human body, a cancer screen has a cost (money, time), but the actual damage created by the cancer increases with time if not treated (the cost of failure is proportional to time). To reiterate, predictive maintenance is used to prevent failures by detecting some type of warning, such as, increased vibration, increased particle count in oil, or increased temperature [1],[2].

Censored Versus Complete Data

If 10 hard disks are tested until all 10 fail, this is a complete data set. If the test is ended before all 10 disks fail, the disks that did not fail are censored. Consider the data in Table 8-1. 8 disk were placed on test stands; 3 of the disk failed, and 5 of the disk were removed from testing without failing.

Table 8-1: An Example of Censored Data

30	60 +
40	60 +
50	60 +
60 +	60 +

Obviously, the sample average and the sample standard deviation for the 3 failed disks can not be used to estimate the parameters of the normal distribution in this case (the sample average equals to (30+40+50)/3 = 40). The time to fail for each of the remaining five disks is greater than 60; the true average is considerably greater than 40. The data in the table above are *right censored*. An item is censored on the right if the failure time is not known, but it is known that the item survived to a known time without failure. If an item is known to be in a failed condition at a specific time, but the exact failure time is not known, this is known as *left censoring*. Single censoring occurs when there is only one censoring point. If 100 transistors are placed onto test stands and the test is terminated after 1,000 hours, there is a single censoring point at 1000 hours. If 20 transistors were removed without failure after 1,000 hours of testing, and another 15 transistors were removed without failure after 1,200 hours of testing, there are 2 censoring points, and the resulting data are multiply censored. If exact failure times are not known, but the numbers of failures in a time interval are recorded, this is known as an *interval or grouped data*.

Weibull distribution

The Weibull distribution is a continuous distribution that was publicized by Waloddi Weibull in 1951. Although initially met with skepticism, it has become widely used, especially in the filed of reliability engineering. The Weibull distribution's popularity resulted from its ability to be used (1) with small sample sizes and (2) based on its flexibility [3],[6]. In addition to being the most useful density function for reliability calculations, analysis of the Weibull distribution provides the information needed for troubleshooting, classifying failure types, scheduling preventive maintenance and scheduling inspections. The Weibull probability density function is depicted in Figure 8-1:

β = the shape parameter

θ = the scale parameter (sometimes expressed as alpha)

δ = the location parameter (sometimes expressed as gamma)

Beta θ, and δ are continuous. The acceptable ranges for these variables are, $0 < \beta < \infty$, $0 < \theta < \infty$, and $-\infty < \delta < \infty$. The estimation of these parameters is not straightforward, and special techniques such as probability plotting, hazard plotting, or maximum likelihood estimation are required to determine the parameters. By altering the shape parameter, β, the Weibull probability density function takes a variety of shapes (see Figure 8-1).

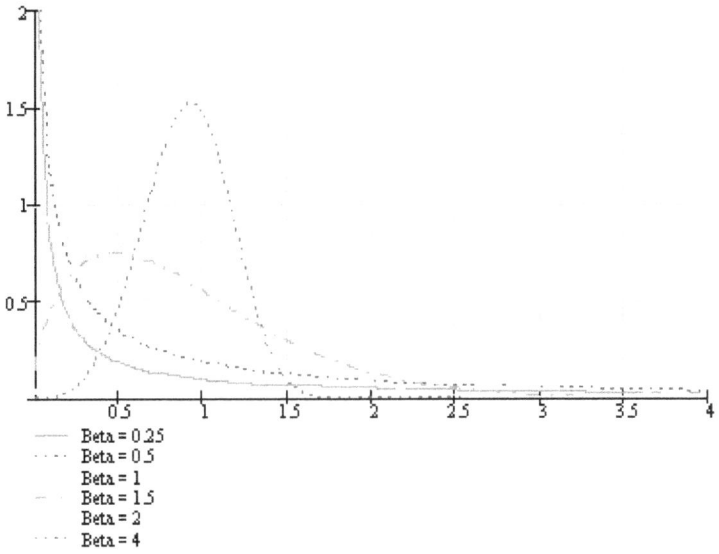

Figure 8-1: Weibull PDF with different values for the shape parameter

It has to be pointed out that several of the probability density functions displayed in Figure 8-1 seem familiar. The Weibull distribution can be used in a wide variety of situations, and dependent on the value of β, equals to (or can approximate) several other distributions. To illustrate:

β = 1   the Weibull distribution is identical to the exponential distribution,

β = 2   the Weibull distribution is identical to the Rayleigh distribution, β = 2.5　　　　the Weibull distribution approximates the log-normal distribution,

β = 3.2 .. 3.6　the Weibull distribution approximates the normal distribution. and

β = 5　　　　the Weibull distribution approximates the peaked normal distribution.

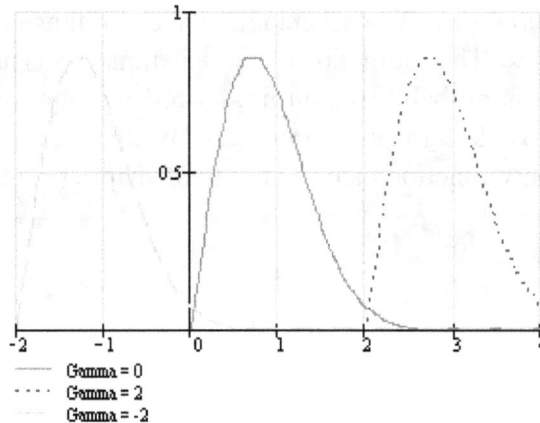

Figure 8-2: Weibull density for Beta = 2 with different location parameters

Because of its flexibility, there are few observed failure rates that can not be accurately modeled via the Weibull distribution. Some specific scenarios are, (1) the breaking strength of components or the stress required to fatigue metals, (2) the time to fail for electronic components, (3) the time to fail for items that wear out (such as tires), and, (4) systems that fail when the weakest component in the system fails. The 4 most widely used methods for determining the Weibull parameters are:

- Maximum Likelihood Estimation,

- Moment Estimation,

- Probability Plotting, and

- Hazard Plotting.

Maximum Likelihood Estimation

Maximum likelihood is the most widely used method for determining the estimators. The method is based on the principle of determining the parameter(s) value(s) that maximize(s) the probability of obtaining the sample data. The likelihood function for a given distribution is a representation of the probability of the sample data of obtaining the sample values. The maximum likelihood estimate theta maximizes the likelihood function. This estimate is asymptotically normal. Often the natural logarithm of the likelihood function is maximized to simplify computations.

Moment estimation

Moment estimation is based on the concept of matching the moments of the sample data with the moments defined by the distribution of interest and its parameters. For example, when estimating the parameters of the 2-parameter Weibull distribution, the first and second moments from the sample data, the sample mean and the sample variance, can be equated as expressions:

Probability Plotting & Hazard Plotting

Probability plotting is a graphical method of parameter estimation. The cumulative distribution function is linearized, usually by a logarithmic transformation, and plotted. The slope and the intercept of the plot provide the information needed to estimate the parameters of the distribution of interest. The median rank is used to estimate the cumulative distribution function, and ranks at user input levels are used to provide confidence intervals for reliability. If manually constructing a probability plot, distribution specific hazard paper is required. By using probability paper, the failure times and cumulative distribution function estimates can be plotted directly. Utilizing mathematical application, specialized graph paper is no longer needed, as using a computer system can make the necessary transformations quickly and easily. Hazard plotting is a graphical method of parameter estimation. The cumulative hazard function is linearized, usually by a logarithmic transformation, and plotted. The slope and the intercept of the plot provide the information needed to estimate the parameters of the distribution of interest. If manually constructing a hazard plot, distribution specific hazard paper is required. By using hazard paper, the failure times and cumulative hazard function estimates can be plotted directly.

Preventive Maintenance

In some cases, it is possible to prevent failures via preventive maintenance [2],[4]. The question is to determine if preventive maintenance is applicable, and if so, how often it should be scheduled. Referring to Figure 8-3, failures can be grouped into 3 categories based on the behavior of the failure rate. Infant mortality failures are characterized by a decreasing failure rate. The hazard function (failure rate) of the Weibull distribution is decreasing if the shape parameterβ < 1.0. Random failures exhibit a constant failure rate; the shape parameter of the Weibull distribution is equal to 1.0.

Wear-out failures have an increasing failure rate; the shape parameter of the Weibull distribution is greater than 1.0. Infant mortality failures are premature failures that can often be prevented by introducing management processes. If infant mortality failures cannot be prevented, a burn-in procedure can be implemented to eliminate failures before the product is shipped. *Preventive maintenance is not applicable for an item with a decreasing failure rate*. Performing preventive maintenance restores the system to its initial state, which has a higher failure rate; preventive maintenance increases the number of failures in this case.

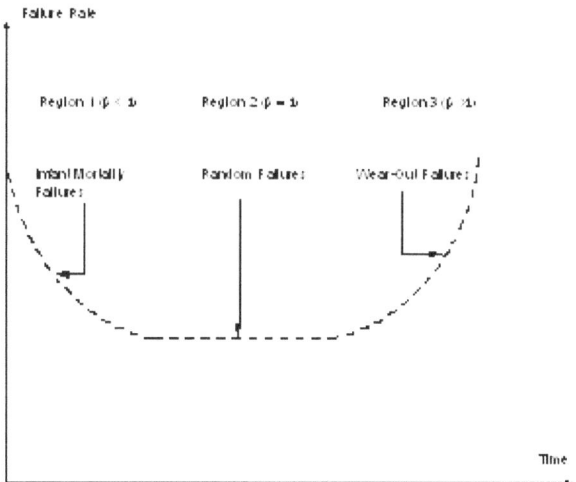

Figure 8-3: Bathtub Curve

Some causes of infant mortality failures are:

- Improper use
- Inadequate materials
- Over-stressed components
- Improper setup

- Improper installation
- Poor quality control
- Power surges
- Handling damage

Random failures cannot be prevented with preventive maintenance. The failure rate is constant, so preventive maintenance has no affect on failures. Reliability can be increased by re-designing the item, or in some cases, by implementing an inspection program. Wear-out failures can be prevented with preventive maintenance. The failure rate is increasing with time, so preventive maintenance restores the system to a state with a lower failure rate. The question is how often should preventive maintenance be scheduled. The time to fail for an item is variable, and can be represented by a probability distribution. Referring to Figure 8-3, the cost of failures per unit time decreases as preventive maintenance is done more often, but the cost of preventive maintenance per unit time increases. There exists a point where the total cost of failures and preventive maintenance per unit time is at a minimum; hence representing the optimum schedule for preventive maintenance [2].

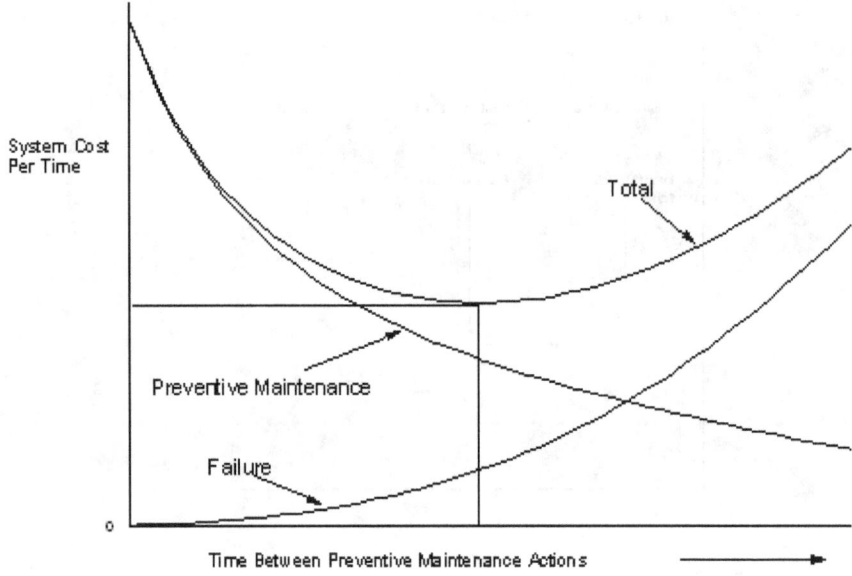

Figure 8-4: Optimum Schedule for Preventive Maintenance

The optimum time between maintenance actions is found by minimizing the total cost per unit time.

The Interrelationship among Reliability, Availability, and Maintainability

System assurance considerations for IT computer systems may include quality assurance, compatibility, reliability, and maintainability. The term system assurance expresses the combined probability that a system or item will perform its required functions for the duration of a specified mission profile, and that the repair action under given conditions and circumstances of usage is carried out within a stated time interval. The system assurance factor is expressed as the factor of reliability and maintainability (see Equation 4). Some key definitions revolving a system assurance study are:

- Failure: An unsuccessful mission, or the circumstance that occurs when the require-ments defined by the mission profile are not met within the mission time.

- Failure Rate: The actual or predicted number of unsuccessful missions divided by the total number of missions. In some scenarios, the failure rate can be expressed as the number of failures per hour, weeks, or months, and is expressed as the reciprocal of MTBF.

- Mission: The end objective desired. For example, this could be defined as adequately cooling the computer room floor so that an over-temp shutdown does not take place. Or, it could be defined as a loss of redundancy.

- Mission Time: The time period over which the mission will take place. The time begins when all systems/components are 100% operational (i.e., failures due to manufacturing defects, poor installation, or improper startup have been repaired) and the system is ready for service. The effect of mission time on reliability is profound. As mission time becomes longer and longer, the probability of success drops. Mission time is usually prescribed by the facility operators based on the economic impact of a failure, and the anticipated life span of the facility.

While system assurance is important in all acquisitions, it is a much more involved process for system-level acquisitions, acquisition of complicated items, and acquisition of items with significant support requirements. The function responsible for achieving the required quality performance includes inspectability, testability, and process control. Figure 8-5 outlines the reliability behavior for a RAID system (expressed via Weibull). The reliability is expressed via the mean time between failure (MTBF) (see Equation 8-1).

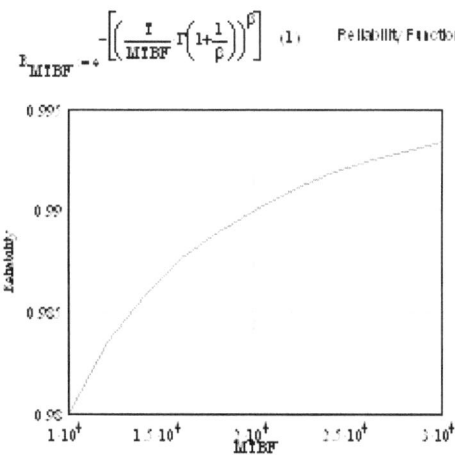

Figure 8-5 Reliability Behavior – RAID system

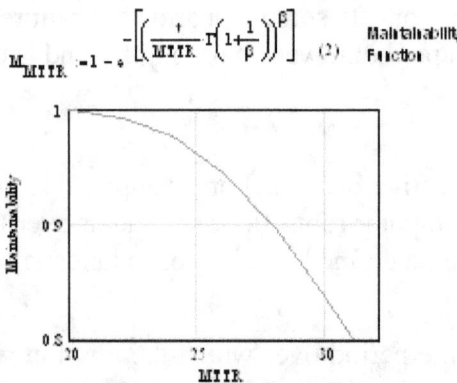

$$M_{MTTR} = 1 - e^{-\left[\left(\frac{t}{MTTR}\cdot \Gamma\left(1+\frac{1}{\beta}\right)\right)^{\beta}\right]} \quad (2) \quad \text{Maintainability Function}$$

Figure 8-6: Maintainability Behavior – RAID system

The maintainability is represented by the mean time to repair (MTTR). The MTTR refers to performing corrective maintenance, which consists of fault isolation and correction (see Equation 8-2).

Availability represents the actual link between the 2 terms reliability and maintainability, as it combines the reliability and maintainability characteristics into a single construct (see Equation 8-3).

$$A_{MTBF, MTTR} = \frac{MTBF}{MTBF + MTTR} \quad (3) \quad \text{Availability Function}$$

$$\%A = R_{30000} \cdot M_{20} \quad (4) \quad \%A = 0.992$$

System Assurance Factor as a combination of MTBF & MTTR

Summary

Preventive maintenance, inspections, and predictive maintenance are all tools that can be used to reduce maintenance expenses. Like any tool, maximum gain is obtained by using these tools correctly. Collecting failure data and optimizing maintenance schedules can make significant financial gains. Further, this chapter elaborated on the interrelationships among reliability, availability, and maintainability. Another focus of this section of the book was on how to mathematically express the system assurance factor.

References

1.   Brick, M., Michael J., (May 1989). "Using Statistical Thinking to Solve Maintenance Problems," Quality Progress

2.   Dodson, Bryan (1994).   Reliability Engineering, Quality Publishing, Tucson, Arizona.

3.   Dodson, Bryan (1994). Weibull Analysis - with software, ASQC, Quality Press, Milwaukee, Wisconsin.

4.   Engineered Software, Inc. (1999) "Using Statistics To Schedule Maintenance"

5.   Hennessy, J., Patterson, D., "Computer Architecture, Quantitative Approach", 3d Edition, Morgan Kaufmann, 2002.

6.   Jain, R., "The Art of Computer System Performance Analysis", John Wiley, 1991

Chapter 9 - Evaluating Systems Stability and the Dynamics of Large Transients

Introduction

Traditionally, availability has been expressed as a binary metric that basically describes whether a system is up or down. A common extension of this definition is to compute the percentage of time that the system is on average available [2]. The thesis made in this chapter is that expressing availability solely as a binary metric is not sensitive enough to disclose the intricacies of a system's potential availability behavior. It is a fact that many of today's computer systems operate in a degraded but operational state, literally a state between being up and down. This scenario can be extended to the point where the degraded state does not cause a down state per se, but has a significant impact on overall systems performance. Circumstances such as a virtual memory trashing, loosing of a disk in a RIAD 5 setup, or the case where the input buffers of a switching element in a communication interconnect are saturated may serve as examples. In all these scenarios, the actual computing environment is still available (from a technical perspective), but operates in a below optimal state [5], [12].

The ramification is that availability has a strong correlation to performance, and should be viewed as a spectrum. The thesis made is that based on the circumstances that surround an analysis, availability may not be defined at either a single point in time or as an average over a certain time-span. The argument made is that when describing availability, it is imperative to characterize the *distribution* rather than the *average*. This approach allows the distinction between a system that is not available for 4 seconds every hour, and another system that is not available for 2 consecutive days each month. Basically, both systems have the same average availability per month, but operate completely different from a user's availability perception. This chapter discusses availability from the perspective of analyzing the dynamics of transitioning from one state to another state and evaluates the impact on computer systems performance, basically focusing on quantifying large transients in computer systems. The project was initiated to determine the actual transition time in a large packet switched network environment. Section 2 elaborates on the concepts of metastability. Section 3 discusses general stability issues in computer systems, and specifically addresses the transition behavior in a Virtual LAN (VLAN) environment [12]. Section 4 introduces the methodology that was being used in this chapter to quantify the actual transition time. The chapter concludes in Section 5 with some remarks on the project's accomplishments.

Metastability

Related to predictions and assessments of availability and reliability is the theory and concepts of metastability and metastable lifetimes [4], [7], [11]. As outlined in the literature, it is feasible to distinguish between two different forms of metastable behaviors in actual computer systems.

- Microscopic Metastability that may occur in VLSI chips (synchronizers and arbiters). A Microscopic Metastability based behavior can lead to a total failure at the system level.

- Macroscopic Metastability that may occur in a higher level of a computer system. and that could potentially lead to a degraded performance behavior.

Microscopic Metastability

Clock synchronization is an essential part of any modern computer system. The technique is required to handle interrupts, to perform bus arbitration, or to ensure handshaking among different hardware components. Basically, any computer system that is composed of multiple subsystems, which are each equipped with different clock generators requires synchronizers to enable the communication among the subsystems [5]. These synchronizers are normally composed of elementary devices known as flip-flops. A digital synchronizer switches between 0 and 1, depending on whether a 0 or a 1 appears on the asynchronous input (relative to another input signal, usually a periodic system clock). A valid synchronization state occurs when the input signal transitions within the specified device parameters. To elaborate, this basically requires that the input signal remains stable within the 'setup to hold time' window as specified by the parameters in the synchronizer. If the signal fails to meet the transition window in a given clock cycle, the output may either resolve to a valid state, or may become metastable.

To reiterate, when the setup and hold criteria's are not being met, the synchronizer transfers into a metastable state where the output pin resides midway between 0 and 1. The length of time a synchronizer may be in the metastable state has no limit or bound. The argument made is that the likelihood of a synchronizer being in a metastable state falls exponentially with time. Hence, only after an infinite time period would the probability be 0 for it to remain metastable. The metastable output may ramify to the inputs of other devices. The ramifications of such microscopic metastability behaviors are either intermittent memory corruption, or in some extreme cases, an actual systems crash. Accommodating metastability normally takes on the form of imposing a sufficient delay to allow any metastable condition to decay into a known state before being propagated. A required delay can be determined if the mean time between failure (MTBF) can be quantified.

Macroscopic Metastability

In computer systems, it is common to have a scenario where for a certain resource, such as physical memory or any communication buffers, an actual queue may represent 2 stable states. One optimal average queue length, and one significantly longer average queue length. The essence of this scenario is that the longer queue length is stable (over a long period of time), and dose not just reflect a brief fluctuation period. As the longer queue length is reached, systems performance will degrade, hence the system is still available, but operates in a degraded (sub-optimal) mode. Based on the thesis made that there are 2 stable queues, the ramification is that there has to be an intermediate (unstable) state in the system. This unstable state is analogous to the microscopic metastability of synchronizers (as discussed in the last paragraph). To reiterate, this behavior can be analyzed in cases where modern memory subsystems are in a state that can be described as 'excessively paging' virtual memory, or where a finite sized communication buffer is being saturated [5]. The argument made is that if feasible, an availability and performance planning study should incorporate an analysis that focuses on determining and quantifying the dynamics of any of these potential transition behaviors.

Transition Dynamics in a VLAN

To substantiate the thesis made in this paper, the analysis is focused on a multistage interconnection network (MIN) that is decomposed into *n*m* switching elements. By partitioning the switching elements, an actual VLAN can be simulated and analyzed.

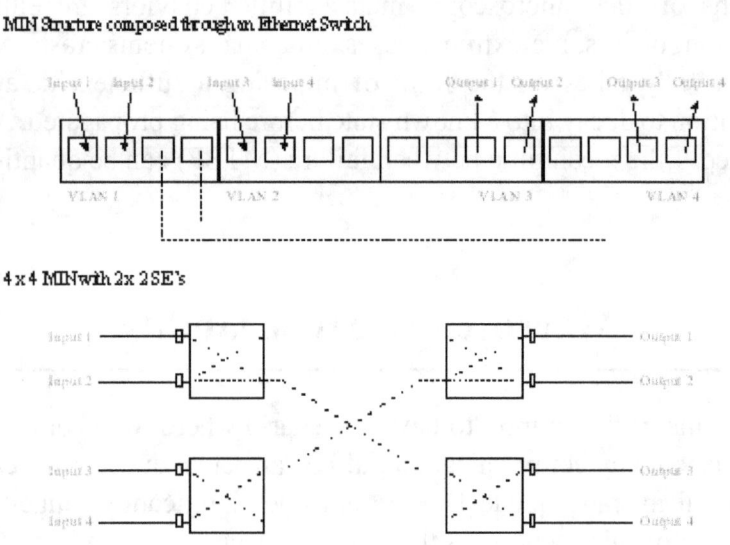

Figure 9-1: MIN and VLAN Components

MIN components are frequently being used to either connect CPU's and memory modules in large-scale multiprocessor systems, or are being deployed as building blocks in high-bandwidth network switches [5], [12]. An advantage of MIN's over a fully meshed crossbar switch is the fact that fewer switching elements are required to build the system, and ergo it is feasible to create rather large networks at a relatively low cost. In general, internal buffers contribute to an increase in performance as the workload is scaled. From a technical perspective, MIN's are composed of several small-sized switching elements that are arranged in stages. As an example, an actual *n*n* MIN consists of *s*s* switching elements that are arranged in *log(n)* stages. All the switching elements forward the packets in a synchronous way (according to an internal clock). Each switching element incorporates a finite buffer that follows the first in first out (FIFO) discipline. The actual buffer is attached to the input port of the switching element, and is being used to store packets that can not be forwarded due to either an output port conflict or a saturated target buffer.

This chapter focuses on a VLAN environment that is based on an Ethernet switch that is partitioned into a 4*4 MIN. The MIN itself is composed of 2*2 switching elements (see Figure 1). From a technical perspective, a VLAN limits the broadcast traffic similar to how a switch limits the collision domain for Ethernet frames; no traffic can cross a VLAN boundary within the actual switch. In other words, a VLAN can be equated to a broadcast domain where the network traffic is disseminated to all the nodes on a shared segment [12]. More specifically, a VLAN can be considered as a group of systems that are not constraint by physical location, enabling a communication behavior as encountered on a LAN segment.

In a queuing model reflecting a single element of the VLAN, the finite size of the internal buffer module can be depicted as a finite population (N), central server system. Additional packets that impact the workload are basically stored in a stable arrival queue. In the case where the workload increases significantly, the system may become unstable to smaller fluctuations, and may transition into a new stable state where the system encounters a performance degradation as the buffer is being saturated. At this stage, the system is still available, but operates in a sub-optimal mode. Assuming that the VLAN system has q □ *[0,N]* requests queued up (which implies that $N - q$ requests remain in an arrival state), the effective arrival rate into the system can be expressed as a linear state dependent function

$\lambda(q) = (N\text{-}q)/ \lambda$ (1):

As depicted in Figure 9-2, the actual throughput is expressed as a non-linear function $\mu(q)$, which incorporates systems activities such as dropped packets, or a conflict situation at the output port. Figure 9-2 reveals that (theoretically) there are three intersection points (Q1, Q2, and Q3) where the arrival rate $\lambda(q)$ equals to the throughput $\mu(q)$ rate [4].

Evaluating Figure 2, if the arrival rate is greater than the throughput rate, there should be more arrivals into the system than departures out of the system, so the queue length will grow. Using Q1 as the baseline, as the queue length increases, a new queue length results that is somewhat greater than Q1 but still less than Q2. This event represents the state where the arrival rate is less than the throughput, ergo the queue length will over time approach Q1. Based on the workload behavior, it is feasible to assume that the queue grows instantaneously to a length greater than Q2, where the arrival rate is greater than the throughput. This behavior drives the system into the third equilibrium point Q3, where again, the arrival rate equals to the throughput [4].

Based on an assumption that the switching element incorporates an infinite queue length, the point of degraded performance Q3 would basically be moved out to infinity. The model depicted would now represent a completely unstable system, compared to a bi-stable system elaborated so far. As discussed in related studies, such a scenario can be modeled as a birth-death process [4], [6], [15].

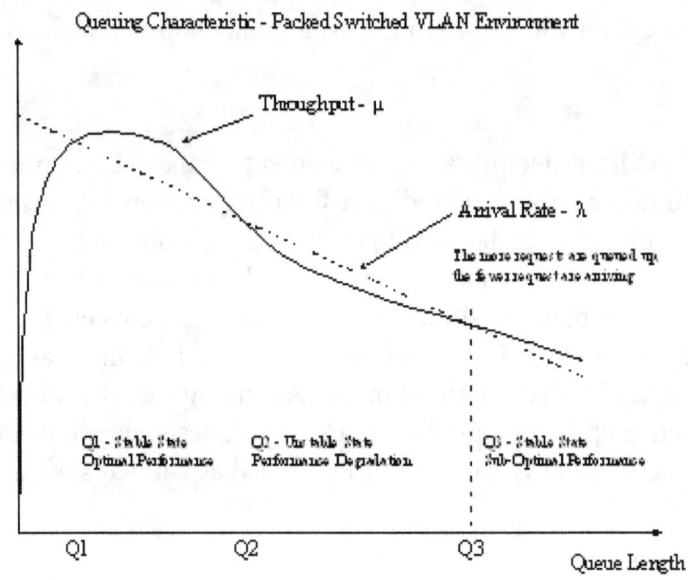

Figure 9-2: Arrival verses Throughput Rate

The resulting Markov chain *[1 .. N]* is represented by a constant arrival rate λ and a departure rate μ, and could represent the toss of an unbiased coin, where the probability of tossing *N* heads in succession (state *N* heads *p(N)* = *p0p1p2...N*, probability *pi* = λ/μ) can be expressed as:

$$p_i = p_0 \left(\frac{\lambda}{\mu}\right)^N \quad (2) \quad i = [1,2 \dots N]$$

To reiterate, if the arrival rate is less than the departure rate *(λ << μ)* the probability of being in a state *N* is small. On the other hand, if λ = μ, the probability of being in a state *N* is a certainty. Further, if λ > μ, the stability point moves towards infinity and outlines that the system becomes unstable [4],[6].

Quantification of the Transition Time

In this chapter, the approach taken to evaluate and analyze the transition time is based on a potential function and a path integral [3], [7]. The analysis focuses on the guidelines outlined and elaborated by Gunther [4] (on metastability and large transients), and incorporates research conducted by Kelly [8] and O'Connell [9] on effective bandwidth and queue lengths, respectively. It has to be pointed out though that the mathematical abstractions presented in this chapter slightly deviate from the discussions in [4],[8], and [9]. A potential function corresponds to a measure of a data structure, whose change after an operation corresponds to the time cost of the actual operation. As discussed in some of the related studies, the value of the potential at any point in the system's time evolution determines the actual *cost* of that state [4], [13], [14]. By utilizing a path integral, this particular cost is described by a quantity labeled the action *S[x(t)]*. As any path *x(t)* is in itself a function of time, the action can be expressed as a function of functions.

Omitting any other external influences, the system will evolve along different paths (with the lowest overall cost or action) between for example points Q1 and Q2 or between points Q2 and Q3 (see Figure 9-2). The goal is to express the dynamics of arbitrary state transitions with mathematical consistency. The interest and focus was on the transient behavior of large queuing systems that can be represented as Markov processes, basically describing a system that was initially in a state *x* at time *t* and underwent a transition to a new state *xi* at a later time *ti* [4], [8]. As the system is stochastic, each of the infinite number of sample paths between the endpoints Q1 and Q2 has an associated probability weighting in the path integral formulation. This behavior is known as the *concept of stochastic sample paths* in a two-dimensional state space *(x,t)*. These paths represent the possible set of transitions a Markov process can experience in both, position and time. As already discussed, each path between Q1 and Q2 has an associated cost, which is denoted by an action *S*. The corresponding probability for each path can be determined as *exp(-NS)*, where for large transients, *N* represents the scale of the system. The argument made is that highly erratic paths between (as an example) the endpoints Q1 and Q2 carry a higher cost, and therefore are rather unlikely to be taken. On the other hand, paths that consider a more direct route between the endpoints are cheaper, and hence have a higher likelihood to be chosen. The cheapest route between the two endpoints is obviously the most direct one. The most direct route can be described as being the path with the *least stochastic fluctuation*, hence it can be considered as the deterministic path. This path is unique and corresponds to the smallest cost (expressed as the least action *S0*). The complete path integral is the functional summation over all the paths between the two endpoints. As *N* increases, only the paths closest to the deterministic path contribute to the path integral. As *N*→∞, the path integral reduces itself to an asymptotic form for a probability *p* that can be expressed as depicted in Equation 3. The actual transition time can now be quantified as the inverse of the probability function *p* as it is expressed in Equation 4.

$$p(Q1,Q2) \sim K e^{-N S_0} \quad (3)$$

$$\tau\left(t_{Q1 \, Q2}\right) \sim K e^{N S_0} \quad (4) \qquad K := \sqrt{N}$$

In the discussed scenario it is necessary to determine the unique value of the action that corresponds to the above elaborated cheapest (deterministic) path between the two endpoints Q1 and Q2 [3], [4], [6]. Considering a birth-death process with a an arrival rate λ and a throughput rate μ, the *generating function* [3] φ(π) can be defined as a path series (Equation 5). The least action *S0* is determined based on the unique solution of *ln* φ(π,x)=0. Therefore, *S0* can be quantified by an equivalent constrained φ(π)=1, which can be solved as a quadratic equation in the variable *e^π*. As the formalism of the path integral theory is based on the calculus of variations, the position of *x* at a particular time *t* can be expressed as *x=x(t)*, whereas the actual velocity of *x* can be defined as *xv=dx/dt*. As *y=xv*, the least action *S0* can be depicted as depicted in Equation 7.

$$\phi(\pi) := 1 + \lambda \cdot \left(e^{\pi} - 1\right) + \mu \cdot \left(e^{-\pi} - 1\right) \quad (5)$$

$$\pi_0 = \ln \frac{y^2 + \sqrt{y^2 + 4\lambda\mu}}{2\lambda} \quad (6)$$

$$\text{where } y = \mu - \lambda$$

$$S_0 = \int_{Q1}^{Q2} \pi(x)\,dx = \ln\left(\frac{\mu}{\lambda}\right) \quad (7)$$

Please see Gunther [4], Kelly [8] and O'Connell [9] for additional mathematical insights into the topic. To visualize large transients in a packet switched network, the chapter evaluated and quantified performance at a *switching element* level in a VLAN environment. The actual experiment was based on *N* statistically independent and identical Markov sources that communicate with the switching element. The sources are either in an active or inactive state, and hence can be modeled as a birth-death process. The rate at which a source becomes either active or inactive is denoted by λ and μ, respectively. The aggregate arrival rate into the system is defined as $N\lambda$, whereas $N\gamma$ depicts the aggregate buffer departure rate. Under a virtual no-load condition, there is no actual buffering in the switching element as the packets are being processed at a rate of $N(\gamma - \lambda)$. As the load increases, buffering at the switching element takes affect and the buffer utilization increases at a rate of $N(\lambda - \gamma)$. Based on this discussion, if the buffer utilization at time t can be denoted as *buf(t)*, the actual *rate of increase* in the buffer utilization *rbuf(t)* can be expressed as *rbuf(t) = N(λ - γ)* [4]. By assuming a mean number of active Markov sources at time t of $0 < x(t) < 1$, the actual source switching rates (state dependent), as well as the equilibrium point e can be defined as:

$$\lambda_{(x)} = N\lambda(1-x)(8)$$

$$\mu_{(x)} = N\mu x (9)$$

$$e = \frac{\lambda}{(\lambda + \mu)} (10)$$

This experiment has a strong correlation to the earlier discussion on metastability, as the equilibrium point e discloses a strong similarity to the intersection point Q1 (in Figure 2). The ramification is that the buffer remains vacant while $x(t) < \gamma$. Assuming a relationship of $e < \gamma < 1$, the system can be considered as remaining in equilibrium at around the intersection point e (see Figure 9-3 & Figure 9-4).

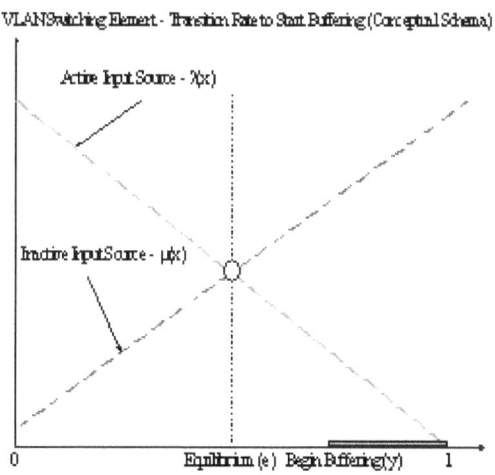

Figure 3: Queuing Characteristics for the VLAN Model

In this particular scenario, there is a single point of equilibrium, hence the analysis is not focused on stability per se, but any fluctuation in $x(t)$ that approaches γ represents a large transient behavior that can be quantified by the path integral equation discussed in this paper. In other words, it is feasible to estimate the transition time to reach γ (where actual buffering in the system starts to occur), as well as the actual buffering probability. Table 1 depicts the transition time and the corresponding probability by for a variety of different workload scenarios representing independent Markov sources *(N)*.

Table 1: VLAN Transition Time and Probability

N	Probability	Transition Time
10	1.47210E-3	6.79410E+3
15	3.88910E-5	3.85710E+5
20	9.68810E-7	2.06410E+7
25	2.33710E-8	1.0710E+9
30	5.52210E-10	5.43310E+10
35	1.28710E-11	2.7210E+12
40	4.69310E-14	1.34810E+14
45	6.79110E-15	6.62610E+15

Note: The actual experiment was conducted with the parameters *(λ)* equal to 0.325 and *(μ)* equal to 0.7.

Modeling the VLAN environment, the conducted experiment nicely outlined the varying transition time values while scaling the number of independent workload sources. Under the same workload conditions, the transition probability depicted an actual reversed behavior. Other techniques that may be utilized to address this issue include *large deviations* or an *exact closed form solution* based approach. See Morrison for further information [16].

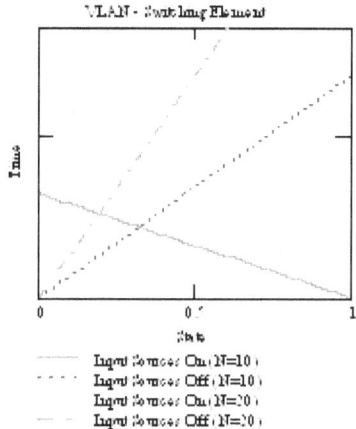

Figure 4: Varying Sample Set (sources)

Summary

This chapter discussed and outlined the stability and performance aspects of computer systems based on a potential function and a path integral based approach, and elaborated that any transition behavior is governed by microscopic effects. Based on the concept of stochastic paths in a two-dimensional state space, the paper focused on the possible set of transitions a Markov process can adapt to in time and position, respectively. The presented mathematical formulization used to quantify the transition time is based on these same concepts. To conclude the work, the paper analyzed and quantified (based on an actual experiment) the transition time, as well as the transition probability of any potential buffering scenarios that may surface in a packet switched VLAN communication environment.

References

10.   Amari, S., Maginu, K., "Statistical Neurodynamics of Associative Memory", Journal on Neural Networks, 1988

11.   Brown, A., *"Towards Availability and Maintainability Benchmarks"*, Masters Thesis, UC Berkley, 2000

12.   Duering, A., Coolen, A., Sherrington, D., "Phase Diagram and Storage Capacity of Sequence Processing Neural Networks", Journal on Physics, Gen. 31, 1998

13.   Gunther, N., *"The Practical Performance Analyst"*, McGraw Hill, 2000

14.   Hennessy, J., Patterson, D., *"Computer Architecture, a Quantitative Approach"*, Morgan Kaufmann, 3d Edition, 2002.

15.   Jain, R., *"The Art of Computer System Performance Analysis"*, John Wiley, 1991

16.   Kawamura M, Okada, M., *"Transient Dynamics for Sequence Processing Neural Networks"*, J. Phys A: Math. Gen., 35, 253 –266, 2002

17.   Kelly, F., "Notes on Effective Bandwidth", University of Cambridge, 1997

18.   O'Connell, N., "Queue Lengths and Departures at Single Server Resources", HP Labs, Bristol, 1995

19.   Patrick, A., Zagrebnov, V., "A Probabilistic Approach to Parallel Dynamics for the Little-Hopfield Model", Journal on Physics, A: Math. Gen. 24, 1991

20.   Schwartz, A., Weiss, A., "Large Deviations for Performance Analysis", Chapman & Hall, 1995

21.   SysKonnect, *"Virtual Networks"* SysKonnect GMBH, Ettlingen, Germany, 2001

22.   Roberts, A., *"Potential function based Analysis of an off line Heap Construction Algorithm"*, Department of Computer Science, University of Sydney, Australia

23.   Tarjan, R., "*Amortized computational complexity*", SIAM Journal on Algebraic and Discrete Methods, 1985.

24.   Zhou, B., Atiquzzaman, M., *"Accurate Analysis of Multistage Interconnection Networks Using Finite Output Buffered Switching Elements"*, IEEE, 1995

25.   Morrison, J., *"Asymptotic Analysis of Data Handling Systems with many Sources"*, SIAM, Journal of Applied Math, 1989

Chapter 10 - A Workload-Dependent Scalability Model for Parallel Applications

Introduction

The degree of parallelism that is achievable in any given application is impacted by a number of factors. Some applications, such as a *sequence comparison* based program, are rather trivial to parallelize as the problem naturally divides into a large number of similar sized tasks. However, for many applications a significant effort is required to achieve a high degree of parallelism. The basic motivation for parallel processing is based on the potential economics of scale offered by an efficiently used parallel system. This chapter proposes a *factorized scaleup model* that allows analyzing the throughput scalability of scientific parallel applications. Aggregate throughput is impacted by modern trends in hardware design that have resulted into a disproportional improvement in CPU speed compared to the actual disk access time. This trend continues into the I/O subsystem, where new disk technologies reveal a disproportional improvement in internal transfer rate compared to the disk seek time. The argument made in this chapter is that the scalability of a parallel scientific application is (next to the encountered workload and communication behavior) heavily impacted by serialization and coherency factors.

High-performance computer systems on the market today can be classified as Symmetric Multiprocessor (SMP), Massively Parallel Processor (MPP), and Non-Uniform Memory Access (NUMA) systems [7]. The major design issue in a SMP environment is that all processors have equal access to the shared resources, namely the shared memory and I/O functionality of the system. The MPP family originated as a straightforward generalization of SMP systems, in which fast workstations are connected to each other. A single MPP component can be partitioned into processors, memory with various access levels including cache subsystems, an interconnect or switch interface, as well as some support hardware. In a classic MPP design, the memory is truly distinct and thus performance is very scalable [13]. This is in strong contrast to the SMP design where the CPU's share the memory subsystem to basically avoid some of the overhead that is associated with internode communication of MPP systems. However, the shared memory design of the SMP family leads to bottlenecks as more processors are added and the bus or crossbar used to access the memory subsystem becomes saturated. Similar to MPP solutions, NUMA systems address the scalability issues found in an SMP environment. The NUMA design introduces additional levels of memory that can be accessed without utilizing any switch fabric. This basic generalization of the SMP architecture is an attempt to regain some degree of scalability by still offering a shared memory solution [7] [12].

This chapter was initiated to substantially improve the accuracy of methods used to evaluate scalability and throughput of parallel scientific applications. Section 2 outlines parallel application performance, basically focusing on programming models and methods, and outlines the issues of performance and scalability. Section 3 discusses the traditional *speedup function* and elaborates on the *efficiency equation*. Section 4 introduces the proposed *factorized scaleup model* and addresses the impact that serialization and coherency issues have on performance. Section 5 discusses the results of actual performance studies conducted on parallel systems. The chapter concludes in section 6 with some remarks on the project's accomplishments.

Parallel Application Performance

Algorithmic constraints may play a decisive role in determining the amount of parallelism possible for any given application. From a software perspective, parallelism within a program may occur at many different levels. A *coarse-grain* design indicates that the units of parallelism are of a significant length of duration relative to the whole program, and usually refers to parallelism implemented at a very high level. A *Fine-grain* design indicates that the units of parallelism are of relatively short duration. It is used to describe loop-level parallelization or data parallelism. As discussed by Koenigs, performance of a real-world application running on a parallel system is a difficult quantity to analyze [9]. Some scientific applications model a complex interplay of phenomena. This may involve different time scales and coupling of physics and chemistry packages in a dynamic framework. On the other hand, commercial Relational Database Management Systems (RDBMS) are normally faced with large working sets, very complex code, and the amount of data that can be shared among the threads is normally harder to partition as compared to a scientific application. The underlying issue for any application is the period of time that is required to solve a given problem. Raw CPU time can not be considered as the main performance indicator, as the CPU time does not take any communication overhead into consideration.

Another factor to consider is that throughput optimization may result in performing some operations multiple times (to avoid the overhead associated with broadcasting the results to too many processors). In some other cases, it is desirable to perform multiple sets of instructions on a single set of data and to retain only one set of results, depending on computations that were being conducted by other threads [13]. Both cases inflate the overhead of computing a result, but do so in the fastest possible manner.

Programming Models and Methods

Parallel programming models are normally designed with very specific hardware architectures in mind [7]. As a result, the variety of parallel programming models is a reflection of the parallel hardware architecture that is available. Although today's systems have converged on a Multiple Instruction Multiple Data Stream (MIMD) style architecture, they completely differ in the way they handle their collective memory. SMP (as well as NUMA) systems define a *single address space*, where a simple memory address is sufficient to locate data in the memory subsystem (utilizing simple load and store instructions). MPP systems on the other hand introduce a *distributed address space* where a remote memory reference requires a translation to the appropriate node. On MPP systems, special protocols are normally utilized to transfer data between the address spaces [11].

For SMP as well as NUMA systems, most programming models include either a *work sharing* or *data parallel* approach. In a *work-sharing* paradigm, a single thread executes until it encounters a parallel construct (such as a parallel loop), at which point the work is divided among a group of threads. After all the threads complete the *processing part of the parallel construct*, control returns to a single thread. On the other hand, in a *data-parallel* approach the parallel constructs are implicit in the array syntax used for specially designed objects. In both models, the location of the data may determine where the execution of the instruction referencing the data item will finally occur [10]. In the case of MPP systems, models designed to work across multiple address spaces are based on *message* and *data passing* libraries. In these models, the threads operate in relative independence and explicitly communicate through function calls to the communication library. Examples of *message-passing* models include the Message Passing Interface (MPI) or the Parallel Virtual Machine (PVM) implementation. Examples of data-passing models include the *shmem* library from Silicon Graphics (SGI) or the *bulk synchronous parallel* library form the University of Oxford [9].

To reiterate, parallelism can either be achieved by utilizing a pipeline or a partitioning based approach. In the case of a pipeline, already processed data is being moved to the next *stage* (as the resource becomes available). Partitioning involves dividing the data into separate sections, processing the sections individually in parallel, and finally combing the output stream [10]. An application that solely utilizes sequential algorithms is normally being scrutinized to ensure the correctness of the produced output. When designing parallel applications, the objective is not only to produce the correct output, but to either decrease the execution time by adding more CPU's or to process a larger data set by utilizing additional resources.

Speedup Function

The characteristics of a parallel application are measured in terms of *speedup* and *scaleup*. For a fixed data set (or problem size), the *speedup* function captures the decrease in execution time that can be obtained by increasing the number of available processors. On the other hand, the *scaleup* function captures how well the parallel algorithm handles larger data sets when additional processors (physical resources) become available. A factor that effects parallel workloads (as well as operating systems) is known as Amdahl's law [1]. Basically, what Amdahl noted in his research was that there is always some irreducible part of an application or algorithm that cannot be decomposed any further to run in parallel. A basic mathematical formulation of Amdahl's law is that the total execution time *t(1)* of any program can be divided into one part that can be processed in parallel and another part that has to be executed sequentially. By defining Ω as the serial time, the parallel time can be expressed as *t(1)(1 - Ω)*. By further defining *p* as the number of processors, the speedup function can be formulated as:

$$s(p) = \frac{t(1)}{t(p)} = \frac{t(1)}{\Omega t(1) + \frac{t(1)(1-\Omega)}{p}}$$

$$s(p) = \frac{p}{p\Omega + 1 - \Omega} = \frac{p}{1 + \Omega(p-1)} \quad (1)$$

$$s(p) = \frac{1}{\frac{1 + \Omega(p-1)}{p}} \qquad \lim_{p \to \infty} \frac{1}{\Omega}$$

In Equation 1, Ω basically depicts the *serialization factor* in Amdahl's law. The speedup calculation is straightforward but reveals some very interesting implications. Suppose that 4% of an algorithm or application is irreducibly serial. Amdahl's law implies that on a 16-CPU system, the obtained speedup equals to 10. Further, Amdahl's law determines that no matter how many processors are configured on the system, with 4% serialization in an algorithm, the maximum possible speedup equals to 25. As the number of processors increases, the parallel portion approaches zero, and the total execution time approaches the serial part (the 4%) of the equation.

The ramification is that even if a lot of processors are configured in a system, the speedup only affects the parallel part of the equation. A variant of the speedup function is known as the efficiency equation. Efficiency is defined as the speedup divided by the number of processors available on the system. In other words, the efficiency of an algorithm can be expressed as the fraction of the total potential processing power that is actually being used. An algorithm with a linear speedup is defined as being 100% efficient.

The Factorized Scaleup Function

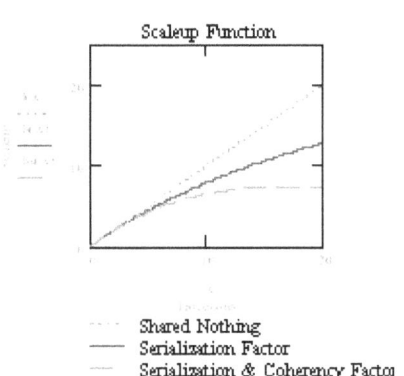

Figure 10-1: Scaleup Function

The traditional scaleup function is defined by DeWitt and Gray [2] as the ability of a *p-times* larger system to perform a *p-times* larger job in the same elapsed time as the original system. The formal scaleup capacity function is defined as the throughput achieved by utilizing *p* processors relative to the resultant throughput when using only one CPU. A scaleup of 1 is defined as being linear, a scaleup of less than 1 implies that there is a reduction in scaleup, and a scaleup of greater than 1 means that the gain is super-linear. Theoretically, if there is no contention among the CPU's (and the system does not encounter any coherency issues), the scaleup will be linear. In such a (theoretical) case, the throughput will increase in direct proportion to either the number of CPU's or the number of worker threads on the system.

The argument made in this chapter is that the scaleup function is impacted by two (in most cases) related factors that cause a deviation (an actual downward trend) from the liner speedup function. The two factors are defined in this chapter as serialization (or contention) factor α and coherency factor β (Figure 1). Serialization issues may occur simply in the hardware, simply in the software, or as a combination occurring in both resources. The thesis is that without any serialization or contention in the system, it is unlikely (but not impossible) that a coherency issue impacts performance. So it is feasible to proclaim that in most cases there is a direct correlation between factor β and factor α. Further, the argument made is that the communication overhead for these particular parallel applications increases by a factor of *p(p-1)/2* when scaling the number of CPU's. The dynamics of this parallel application behavior can be described as utilizing a *request-reply* communication mechanism where the CPU *interaction overhead* among the threads stabilizes at approximately the number of available communication links.

Next to Amdahl's [1] and Koenigs [9] [10] work, this chapter was influenced by research conducted by DeWitt [2] who elaborated on scalability issues within parallel database systems, and Gustafson [5] who challenged Amdahl's Law in conjunction with MIMD systems. Further, this chapter researched and analyzed Eager's [3] work on speedup verses efficiency issues, and studied Gunther's [4] approach to evaluating the scaleup efficiency for commercial workloads. Based on the conducted research, the *factorized scaleup function* Φ introduced in this chapter is defined in Equation 2 (for *p>1* and $\alpha>0$) as:

$$\Phi(p) = \frac{p}{1+\alpha\left[(p-1)+\beta\frac{p(p-1)}{2}\right]} \quad (2)$$

if $\alpha = 0$ (no serialization)

$$\Phi(p)_c = \frac{p}{1+\left[\beta\frac{p(p-1)}{2}\right]} \quad (3)$$

$$\Gamma(p) = \frac{p}{1+\alpha(p-1)} \quad (4)$$

An important aspect of the presented model is that based on the fact that the coherency factor β increases in a quadratic fashion (proportional to the number of processors available), the factorized scalability function determines a definite throughput maximum on any given system. The maximum system throughput is achieved with fewer processors as β increases. This chapter further argues that as β→α a more 'aggressive' scaleup model Γ is introduced that *resembles* Amdahl's law, and is referenced here as the *Amdahl Scaleup model*.

Equation 4 incorporates the serialization factor α but omits any coherency aspects on a system (Figure 1). The thesis made in this chapter is that first, the potential degree of contention as well as the potential degree of coherency that may exist in a parallel environment impacts the scalability of a parallel application. Second, for most parallel systems, coherency issues on SMP nodes almost always affect performance. Third, the factorized scaleup function outlines that there is most likely a maximum capacity on a system.

Serialization Issues on Parallel Systems

Figure 2 and 3 outline the effects that a serial section in an algorithm (or application) has on performance. The part of the application that can be executed in parallel can be reduced in proportion to the number of CPU's available to process the workload. The part of the application (in this case the critical section) that causes the serialization effect remains unchanged as only one CPU can process the serial work at any given time.

The ramification is that as more CPU's are available to process the parallel portion of the application (if that is feasible from an application design standpoint), the serial portion of the application becomes the dominating factor in regards to total execution time [13]. The conclusion is that the serial section of an application (in conjunction with any coherency issues that may exist) is responsible for the downward trend in the scaleup curve (Figure 1).

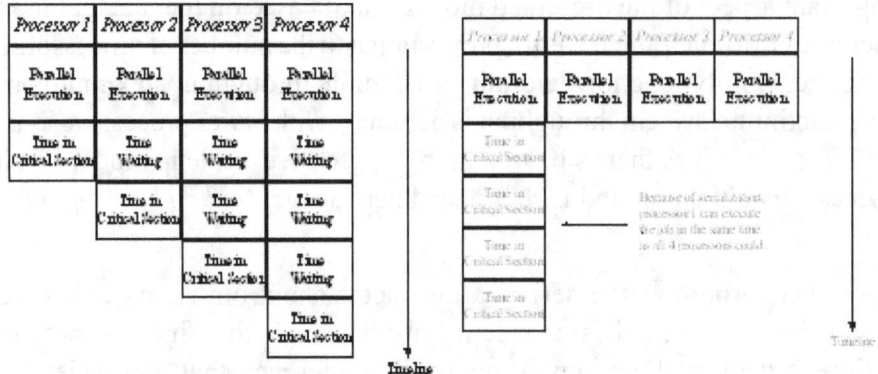

Figure 10-2 & 10-3: Contention for a Shared Resource

As outlined in Figure 2, in a first phase all CPU's are processing a specific section of the application in parallel. If the work is perfectly distributed among all the available CPU's, the application threads will reach the critical section (the shared resource) simultaneously, causing a serialization in the processing flow. The implication is that a single processor is capable of handling the serial workload as efficiently as all four available processors combined. At the point where the critical section is reached, there is no performance gain in scaling the number of CPU's (Figure 3). The specific number of processors used in this example is indeed an artifact of the diagram. But performance and scalability *obstacles* like this are a general phenomenon. The issue is how much time is spent in the serial code, compared to how much time is spent by the processors executing the parallel sections of an application. As a basic rule, given *p* processors, as soon as *(p * serial time) > parallel time*, there is no need (no actual performance gain) to configure more processors on the system.

Coherency Issues on Parallel Systems

The second factor that impacts the shape of the scaleup curve is closely related to the serialization or contention issues discussed in the last few paragraphs. It is only one part of the overall *performance equation* to design and implement a system that processes an application or algorithm as efficiently as possible. A far more serious scenario is described by the correctness (or incorrectness) of the results produced by an application or an algorithm. On parallel systems, multiple copies of the same data are potentially maintained in different hardware caches of the processors. The sharing of data in multiple cache subsystems is referred to as the *cache coherency* problem. On an SMP, the system has to provide a coherent, uniform view of the memory subsystem to all the processors, despite the presence of a per processor local cache subsystem [13]. The argument is that keeping the cache subsystems in sync affects performance as the additional time necessary to fetch data from either another cache or the memory subsystem impacts the transaction latency.

This effect has to be taken into consideration when determining the scaleup of a system, as it will result in a more dramatic performance degradation when compared to the *shared nothing* scaleup curve in Figure 10-1. The thesis made in this research is that without any serialization or contention in the system there is most likely no coherency issue. One exception where the system may encounter a coherency situation without necessarily being confronted with serialization is known as *false sharing*. False sharing arises from the use of an invalidation-based coherence algorithm with a single valid bit per block in the cache tag [7]. False sharing occurs when a block is invalidated because some word in the block, other than the one being read, is written. If the modified word is actually used by the processor that received the invalidate, then the reference was a true sharing reference and would have caused a miss, independent of the block size or position of the words. If the word that is written and the word read are different, and the invalidation does not cause the communication of a new value but an extra cache miss, then the result is a false sharing miss (see Equation 3). In a false sharing miss scenario, the block is shared, but no word in the cache is actually being shared.

I/O Scaleup Analysis on an MPP System

The next few paragraphs outline an actual performance study conducted on an IBM RS/6000 SP MPP cluster. The system was configured with 2 SP Switch2 adapters per node, and utilized a single IBM Virtual Shared Disk (VSD) I/O server that was configured with 96 RAID-5 units (4+P). The goal of this experiment is to discuss the potential of the proposed factorized scaleup model (in regards to performance and capacity planning), as well as to evaluate the throughput based on the two parameters α and β. The benchmark used in this study simulates a scientific parallel application where the number of threads that are involved in the communication process stabilizes at around the number of available communication links. The benchmark measures the aggregate I/O throughput utilizing IBM's General Parallel File System (GPFS) as the data repository [6]. The benchmark scales the number of GPFS compute nodes (increasing the number of available CPU's by 16 per added node), as well as the aggregate workload that has to be processed on the system. Per GPFS compute node, four concurrent worker threads are being used where each thread is processing 512MB of data. In an MPP environment like this, it would be a daunting task to utilize a standard queuing model to characterize the throughput [8].

Table 10-1: Measured GPFS Read Throughput (MPP system)

Number of Nodes (p) 16 CPU's per Node	Aggregate Throughput (in MB/second)
1	349.5
2	586.9
4	650.9
6	696.0
8	705.0
12	712.1
16	716.7
24	722.4
28	721.1

In Equation 2, $\Phi(p)$ depicts the normalized throughput or capacity for p nodes. The first step in evaluating the scaleup function consists of calculating (for every data point) the relative capacity Φ, the efficiency factor δ, as well as the inverse efficiency factor ε. The relative capacity Φ is determined as the measured throughput for p compute nodes $\Phi(p)$ divided by the measured throughput for one compute node $\Phi(1)$.

Table 10-2: Capacity Ratios

p	Φ	$\delta = \Phi/p$	$\varepsilon = p/\Phi$
1	1	1	1
2	1.68	0.84	1.19
4	1.86	0.47	2.15
6	2.0	0.33	3.0
8	2.02	0.25	3.96
12	2.04	0.17	5.88
16	2.05	0.13	7.81
24	2.07	0.09	11.59
28	2.06	0.07	13.59

(Non-linear) Regression Analysis

The second step in this performance analysis consists of transforming the factorized scaleup function into a standard quadratic equation as depicted in Equation 5. This transformation is necessary, as it is impossible to directly perform a regression analysis on the proposed scaleup function. Ultimately, it is necessary to establish a connection between the two factors α and β (see Equation 2), and the three coefficients *a, b*, and *c* (see Equation 5). As a non-linear regression analysis is not a simple *curve fitting* exercise, the degree of freedom in Equation 5 has to be constrained to fit the number of parameters defined in Equation 2 [8]. In order to achieve that goal, the regression has to be constraint in a form that there are only 2 coefficients, and that their values are always positive. This is accomplished by transforming Equation 2 as:

$$y = ax^2 + bx + c \quad (5)$$

$$\frac{P}{\Phi} = 1 + \alpha \left[(p-1) + \beta \frac{p(p-1)}{2} \right] \quad (6)$$

$$Y = \frac{P}{\Phi} - 1 \quad X = p - 1$$

$$Y = \alpha \frac{\beta}{2} x^2 + \frac{\alpha \beta + 2\alpha}{2} x \quad (7)$$

The right side of Equation 7 depicts a simple, second-degree polynomial and so establishes a connection to the quadratic equation outlined in Equation 5. By defining *Y* and *X*, Equation 6 can be transformed into Equation 7 (an actual *parabola* that very much resembles Equation 5). The only difference is that there is no *c* coefficient defined in Equation 7, in other words the transformation was accomplished by setting the *intercept parameter c* to zero. The implication is that the regression analysis now can be performed on the two newly defined variables *X* and *Y*.

Table 10-3: Non-Linear Regression Analysis on X and Y

p - 1	P/Φ - 1
0	0
1	0.19
3	1.15
5	2.0
7	2.96
11	4.88
15	6.81
23	10.59
27	12.59

Conducting this research, it was determined that the relationship between the parameters α and β from Equation 2, and the coefficients *a* and *b* from Equation 5 can be expressed as:

$$\alpha = \frac{2a}{b-a} \quad (8) \qquad \beta = \frac{2a}{\alpha} \quad (9)$$

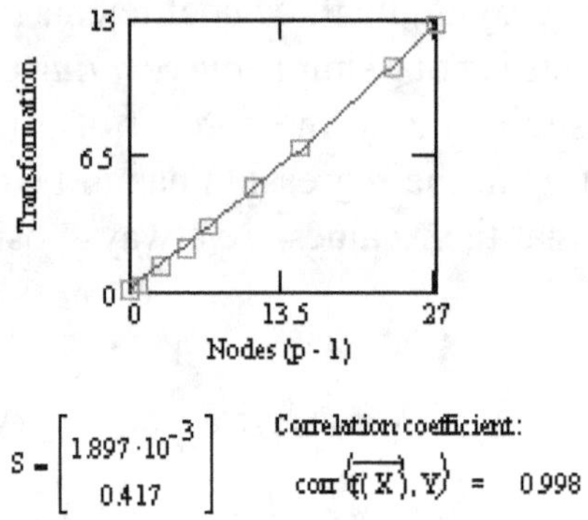

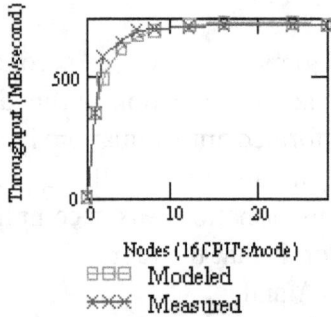

$$S = \begin{bmatrix} 1.897 \cdot 10^{-3} \\ 0.417 \end{bmatrix} \qquad \text{Correlation coefficient:} \\ \text{corr}(t(X), Y) = 0.998$$

Figure 10-4: Regression-Fit to the Parabolic Transformation

Figure 10-5: Factorized Scaleup

Based on these newly defined relationships, it is possible to calibrate the model and to quantify the coefficients *a* and *b*. Mathcad was being used throughout this study to conduct all the computations, as well as to perform the actual non-linear regression analysis. As determined by the factorized scaleup model, for this experiment the parameters *a* and *b* equal to 0.00189 and 0.417, respectively. The correlation coefficient equals to 99.8%, and basically depicts the percentage of variability in the data that is accounted for by the factorized scaleup function. This implies that only 0.2% of the data is unaccounted for by the proposed model, a very encouraging low number. The parameters α and β can now be determined by using the inter-relationships defined in Equations 8 and 9. The resulting values for the parameters α and β equal to 0.415 and 0.0091, respectively. The last step necessary to conclude the regression analysis is to generate the entire factorized scaleup curve based on Equation 2.

The conducted study reveals that the serialization factor α equals to 41.5%, whereas the coherency factor β equals to 0.9%. The analysis further reveals that for up to 8 GPFS nodes, the serialization factor (the actual serial contention) is slightly higher than predicted, and that for more than 8 GPFS nodes, the serialization factor is slightly lower than what has been modeled.

Table 10-4: GPFS Read Throughput (MPP System)

Nodes	Measured Throughput (MB/second)	Modeled Throughput (MB/second)
1	349.5	349.5
2	586.9	492.8
4	650.9	615.1
6	696.0	671.0
8	705.0	697.3
12	712.1	719.9
16	716.7	728.4
24	722.4	723.8
28	721.1	717.9

When scaling the number of GPFS compute nodes (the actual workload), the SP Switch2 interconnect configured in this SP MPP cluster becomes the bottleneck [8]. Increasing the workload causes contention for this shared resource. The measured (as well as the modeled) performance data reveals that there is virtually no throughput gain when increasing the workload beyond 8 GPFS client nodes (Table 4).

I/O Scaleup Analysis on an SMP System

To further evaluate the potential of the proposed factorized scaleup model, the next experiment conducted in this chapter is focused on a single GPFS application node (an actual SMP system), and evaluates the I/O throughput scalability when increasing the number of worker threads (an actual workload increase).

The benchmark program used in the second experiment scaled the number of GPFS worker threads from 1 to 16 while keeping the number of CPU's fixed at 16 processors. The study used one VSD I/O server that was configured with 96 RAID-5 (4+P) units as a backing store. Utilizing the same factorized scaleup model, the measured throughput numbers are summarized in table 5 [8]. The model calculates a correlation factor of 99.9%. The parabolic transformation discloses values of 0.011 and 0.237 for the coefficients *a* and *b*, respectively. The parameters α and β (as determined by the model) equal to 0.227 and 0.097 respectively. The very high correlation factor in conjunction with a low description error is an encouraging confirmation of the validity of the modeling approach taken in this study.

The main performance bottleneck for this particular (single SMP node) configuration is the CPU copy rate, which stabilizes around 430 MB/second for a multiple CPU SMP system. The analysis reveals that for 1, 2, 4, and 16 worker threads, the serialization factor (the actual serial contention) is slightly higher than predicted, and that for 8 worker threads the serialization factor is slightly lower than what has been modeled (see Figure 6). The measured as well as the modeled performance data reveals that the peak aggregate throughput is achieved with 8 worker threads, and that for the 16 thread workload the actual aggregate I/O throughput starts to retrograde.

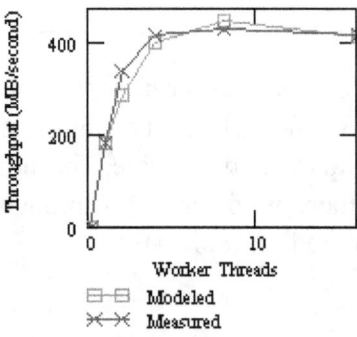

Figure 10-6: Factorized Scaleup (SMP node)

NAS Scaleup Analysis on a Linux Cluster

The next experiment conducted for this chapter utilized a subset of the NAS parallel benchmark, analyzing the scalability of the FT and LU Kernels on a Linux cluster. The NAS parallel benchmark set consists of eight programs designed to evaluate the performance of parallel super-computers [7] [15]. The benchmarks are derived from computational fluid dynamic (CFD) applications. The test environment consisted of a 16-node Linux 2.2.14 cluster. Each node in the cluster was equipped with dual Pentium III 450MHz CPU's and 256 Mbytes of memory. The nodes were interconnected through Dolphin D311/D312 32bit 33MHz SCI-PCI cards, arranged in a 4x4 torus. The actual performance measurements are available from Scali [14]. The NAS FT kernel implements the time integration of a three-dimensional partial differential equation utilizing Fast Fourier Transformation. For every time-step along the way, an actual data exchange is being performed, where each processor has to send a subset of its data to every other processor in the cluster. The benchmark scaled the number of nodes in the cluster from 1 to 16, whereas each node was running two processes.

The model revealed a correlation factor of 1 for the FT Kernel benchmark. The parameters α and β (as determined by the factorized model) equal to 1.1 and 0.016, respectively. The high serialization factor is expected as the benchmark simulates a very high inter-processor communication load. For the FT Kernel, the average description error is less than 2.2%. The factorized scaleup model slightly understates the scaleup for the 2-node configuration, and slightly overstates the scaleup for the 4, 8, and 16-node setup (see Figure 10-7).

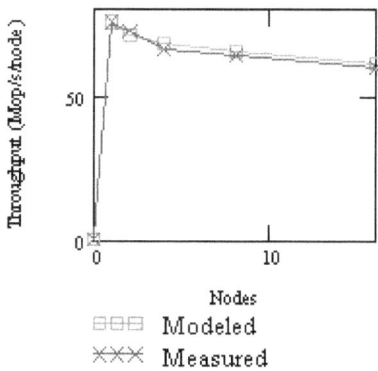

Figure 10-7: Factorized Scaleup (FT Kernel)

The NAS LU Kernel benchmark on the other hand executes a triangular factorization of a matrix. The benchmark operates on a large number of very small messages. The benchmark conducted on the Linux cluster scaled the number of nodes from 1 to 16, whereas each node was running two processes (see Figure 10-8).

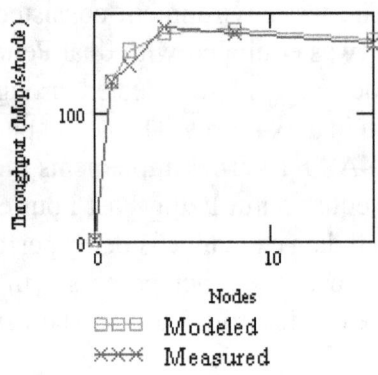

Figure 10-8: Factorized Scaleup (LU Kernel)

Modeling the LU Kernel resulted into a correlation factor of 1. The conducted parabolic transformation revealed values of 0.0073 and 0.685 for *a* and *b*, respectively. The resulting serialization factor equals to 0.664, whereas the coherency factor equals to 0.022. The factorized scaleup model is basically in line with the measurements taken on the Linux cluster, slightly overstating the scaleup for the 2-node configuration (with an average description error of less than 3.6%). For both NAS benchmarks, a correlation factor of 100% implies that all the measured data is accounted for by the factorized scaleup function

Summary

This chapter introduced a factorized scaleup model that is based on two parameters (α and β) which represent the serialization and the coherency factor, respectively. The model can be used to evaluate the scalability of certain parallel applications, and can be utilized as a powerful capacity-planning tool. The factorized scaleup model predicted a read throughput of 723.8 MB/second for 24 GPFS nodes, and 717.9 MB/second for 28 GPFS nodes. Actual measurements taken afterwards on the GPFS MPP cluster (see Section 5 for the benchmark description) revealed read throughput numbers of 722.4 MB/second and 721.1 MB/second, respectively. This results into a *model prediction error* of only 0.2% for the 24 node and 0.44% for the 28 node configuration. The proposed model further outlines that based on the communication behavior of the parallel application, there is a potential maximum to the throughput scalability that can possibly be achieved on any given parallel system. This is in strong contradiction to the normally very optimistic scaleup functions that are being used for capacity planning. Figure 9 shows the impact of ignoring the coherency factor while analyzing the scaleup for the GPFS MPP benchmark (see Table 10-1). For this particular scientific workload, the Amdahl Scaleup model (where the coherency factor β is set to zero) substantially overstates the scaleup as the workload is being increased.

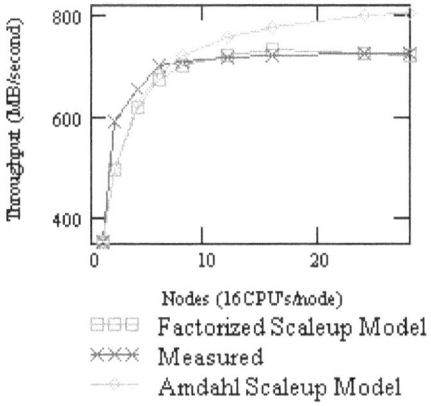

Figure 10-9: Amdahl's Scaleup Model

Amdahl's scaleup function represents a *broadcast based CPU interaction protocol* where a single CPU broadcasts a message to every other CPU in the configuration (and hence simulates a different application behavior). In Amdahl, the CPU interaction overhead grows less aggressively compared to the *request-reply* based approach incorporated in the factorized model, and basically reaches an asymptote as the capacity is being increased. Unfortunately, parallel applications that reveal such a high degree of parallelism are very difficult to develop, the data set is convulsive to partition, and so are rather unusual. A matrix manipulation based application would be an example of a program that could potentially reveal such a high degree of parallelism. This study analyzed several parallel scientific applications that all revealed a request-reply based CPU interaction profile, where basically the CPU communication overhead stabilizes at approximately the number of available processor communication links on SMP systems, or the number of node interaction links on MPP clusters.

In this chapter, the conducted experiments revealed the potential of the new model, outlined its accuracy, and showed that the factorized scaleup function is universally applicable to SMP systems and MPP clusters, respectively. A very important artifact of the presented model is that it does not make any reference to the operating system, the system interconnect, or the system architecture that is being used in the performance analysis or capacity study. These very complex details that normally have a profound impact on the complexity of a performance analysis are incorporated into the two parameters α and β. The proposed model shows a very high degree of accuracy in test cases where the benchmark scaled the number of nodes and CPU's (an increase in physical resources), as well as when the benchmark scaled the number of worker threads on a single node (an increase in a logical resource).

References

26.   Amdahl, G., *"On the Validity of the Single Processor Approach to Achieving Large-Scale Computing Capabilities"*, Proceeding of the AFIPS Conference, 1967

27.   DeWitt, D., Gray, J., *"Parallel Database Systems: The Future of High Performance Database Systems"*, 1992

28.   Eager, D., Zahorjan, J., Lazowska E., *"Speedup verses Efficiency in Parallel Systems"*, IEEE, 1989

29.   Gunther, N., *"The Practical Performance Analyst"*, McGraw Hill, 2000

30.   Gustafson, J., *"Reevaluating Amdahl's Law"*, Communication of the ACM, Volume 31, February 1988

31.   Heger D., Shah, G., *"GPFS 1.4 for AIX – Architecture and Performance"*, IBM White Paper, Poughkeepsie, NY, 2001

32.   Hennessy, J., Patterson, D., *"Computer Architecture, Quantitative Approach"*,

Morgan Kaufmann, 96.

33.   Jain, R., "*The Art of Computer System Performance Analysis*", John Wiley, 1991

34.   Koenigs, A. "*Industrial Strength Parallel Computing*", Morgan Kaufmann, San Francisco, 2000

35.   Koenigs, A. "*Parallel Application Performance*", Lawrence Livermore National Laboratory, 1998

36.   Shah, G., Nieplocha, J., Mirza, J., Kim, C., Harrison, R., "*Performance and Experience with LAPI*", International Parallel Processing Symposium, Orlando, FL, 1998

37.   Stone, H., "*High Performance Computers*", Addison-Wesley, First Edition, New York, NY, 1991

38.   Pfister, G. F., "*In Search of Clusters*", Second Edition, Prentice Hall PTR, NY, 1998.

39.   Scali "*NAS Parallel Benchmarks*", http://www.scali.com/performance/scali.html, 2000.

40.   Woo, A., Bailey, D., Harris, T., Saphir, W., Wijngaart R., "*The NAS Parallel Benchmarks*", NAS-95-020, December, 1995

Chapter 11 - Deterministic Stochastic Petri Net I/O Performance Quantification

Introduction

The goal of this chapter was to mathematically abstract, evaluate, and quantify the relative performance behavior of different I/O subsystem designs in a Linux 2.6 centric I/O framework. The focus was on RAID cache techniques, I/O request coalescing, and queuing behaviors in a heterogeneous workload environment. While the generic model was based on the entire Linux 2.6 I/O stack, a specific emphasis was on the RAID cache subsystem. The introduced deterministic stochastic Petri Nets (DSPN) address the sensitivity of the I/O stack in general, and the RAID cache architecture in particular, on the encountered traffic intensity and burstiness of the I/O requests. The study takes different cache scenarios, queuing behaviors, coalescing efforts, and hardware latency issues into consideration while abstracting the I/O framework.

Over the last decade, the I/O subsystem framework has become considerably more complex. Contemporary I/O stacks include software, hardware, as well as firmware support for features such as request coalescing, adaptive prefetching, automated invocation of direct I/O, or asynchronous write-behind techniques. Incorporating large cache subsystems on a memory, RAID cache controller, as well as physical disk layer allows for a very aggressive utilization of these I/O optimization techniques [13],[21]. The interaction of the different optimization techniques is neither well understood nor has been analyzed and quantified in an in-depth manner. The argument made is that that there is a vast need for performance models that can predict the behavior of any given I/O subsystem infrastructure, which is configured in a given way, and is subject to a given workload. A predictive model provides the analyst with the ability to explore the consequences of multiple design alternatives and architectural trade-off's, without having to physically implement the rather costly I/O infrastructure. The main contribution of this chapter is an adaptive, DSPN based model that allows predicting the I/O performance under different workload conditions and hardware configurations. The models can be utilized very early on in the systems design stage, providing valuable information on the anticipated I/O behavior.

In general, DSPN's are utilized to facilitate and formulate the high-level modeling abstractions of discrete-event systems that consist of exponential and deterministic subtasks [15],[23]. In most circumstances, while the encountered I/O traffic is rather bursty (stochastic), the latency of the cache-hit scenarios (at a memory as well as a RAID subsystem level) can be described as being deterministic. Therefore, the consolidation of stochastic and deterministic timing behaviors in a DSPN framework supports the application of this particular approach in this chapter to quantify I/O performance. From a RAID cache perspective, the chapter discusses the relative performance behavior of a write-through and a write-back implementation [24], respectively. For both RAID cache solutions, the chapter evaluates the performance under various workload scenarios. The remainder of this paper is structured such as that Section 2 briefly introduces the concepts employed by Petri Nets (PN), focusing on the specific features of DSPN's, and addressing the PN's *state space* issue. Section 3 elaborates on the Linux 2.6 I/O stack, and introduces the write-back and the write-through RAID cache architecture. Section 4 describes and elaborates on the proposed DSPN models. Section 5 discusses the results of the study, whereas Section 6 formulates the conclusions and addresses some future work items.

Deterministic Stochastic Petri Nets

A Petri Net model represents a graphical abstraction of a system, and basically utilizes 2 types of nodes (*places* and *transitions*) as the building blocks [5],[6],[12]. Places represent states, whereas transitions depict the action being executed in the system. From a graphical perspective, circles represent the places, whereas the transitions are depicted as bars. The arcs of the graph are classified (in respect to the transitions) as *input, output*, and *inhibitor* arcs. The input arcs are arrow-headed arcs directed from places to transitions. The output arcs are arrow-headed arcs going from transitions to places. The inhibitor arcs are circle-headed arcs directed from places to transitions, and are used to enforce rules on which transition can fire under certain workload conditions. All these arcs are directed. Multiple arcs among places and transitions are permitted, and are explicated with a number specifying the multiplicity factor. Places can contain tokens that are depicted as black dots within places. The state of a PN is called the *marking*, and is defined by the number of tokens held in each place. According to classical automata theory, there is a notion of initial state (initial marking) in PN's. The number of tokens initially configured in the PN's places can be graphically represented by symbols that are considered parameters of the model [23].

An initial marking of one or more parameters represents the family of markings that can be obtained by assigning different legal values to the parameters. To reiterate, in

PN modeling, places represent conditions, whereas transitions represent events. A token arriving at a place is interpreted as a true condition. The dynamic evolution of the PN's marking is governed by transition firing mechanisms that create and destroy tokens. An *enabling rule* and a *firing rule* are associated with transitions. The enabling rule states the conditions under which transitions are allowed to fire. The firing rule defines the marking modification produced by the transition firing. Both, the enabling and the firing rule are specified through arcs. In particular, the enabling rule involves input and inhibitor arcs, while the firing rule depends on input and output arcs. A transition is enabled if (and only if) each input place contains a number of tokens greater than or equal to a given threshold, and each inhibitor place contains a number of tokens strictly smaller than a given threshold. These thresholds are defined by the multiplicity factor of the arcs. When transition *t* fires, it deletes from each place (in its input set *t*) as many tokens as represented by the multiplicity factor of the arc connecting that place to *t* [16],[25]. At the same time, it adds to each place in its output set *t* as many tokens as represented by the multiplicity factor of the arc connecting *t* to that place.

In general, PN's have gained substantial popularity over the years, mainly because of their applicability to modeling and analyzing concurrent systems [9],[23]. However, the actual concept of time is not explicitly provided in the PN framework, which limits their usefulness for real-time systems. The time related extension of PN's primarily imposes additional timing constraints onto transitions or places. The imposed timing constraints can be represented as constants or functions. Timed PN's associate a finite fire duration with each transition. Timed PN's are capable of specifying timing requirements for the components of a system with a fixed execution or delay time factor. As an example, a constant is used to represent a single delay, whereas a function is utilized to describe a time pair consisting of a lower and an upper bound. Other functions incorporated into PN's represent timing constraints as a probability function of the transition-firing rate. Timed PN's that assign an exponentially distributed time component to transitions, or in other words, systems where the time represents the delay between enabling and firing of a transition, are known as Stochastic Petri Nets (SPN's) [6].[25]. SPN's are commonly used for simulation-based performance evaluations. The performance is evaluated by determining a minimum cycle time for completing a firing sequence (where each transition fires at least once) that leads back to the initial marking, i.e. finding the minimum cycle time for the execution of a periodic process. As such, each timed transition can be used to model the execution of an activity in a distributed environment, and all activities execute in parallel (unless otherwise specified by the SPN structure) until they complete. At completion, these activities produce a local change of the system state that is specified by the interconnection of the transition to input and output places. The firing of a transition may describe either the completion of a time-consuming activity, or the verification of a logical condition [25].

Deterministic Stochastic Petri Nets (DSPN's) augment the discussed framework by simulating exponential as well as deterministic events. Therefore, in a DSPN setup, three types of transitions are defined. (1) Immediate transitions that fire without any delay are represented as thin bars. (2) Exponential transitions are depicted as empty bars, and represent the firing criteria triggered after an exponentially distributed delay with a given mean value has expired. (3) Deterministic transitions that are graphically expressed as black bars, and basically fire after a given constant delay factor expired. The firing of an immediate transition takes precedents over the firing of any timed transition. Firing weights are associated with immediate transitions to arbitrate the probability of firing, and hence to circumvent any potential conflicts. The firing delays of the exponential and deterministic transitions, respectively, as well as the firing weights of the immediate transitions may depend on the current marking of the DSPN. To reiterate, marking states that enable immediate transitions are passed through in zero time and are referred to in the literature as *vanishing* states [25]. On the other hand, the marking states representing the timed transitions are labeled as *tangible* states. In general, the Poisson arrival process of a Markov modulated system can be described as a DSPN [5],[6]. As a process spends zero time in a vanishing state, these states do not contribute to the time behavior of the system and hence, can be omitted from the Markovian chain. It has to be pointed out though that while stochastic PN based Markov modeling solutions may represent a powerful and generic approach to evaluating the performance and dependability of many different systems, state space size issues have to be addressed accordingly [26]. In other words, as the size of the state space grows exponentially with the systems complexity, very large Markovian models may not be suitable for being abstracted and simulated in most available PN applications and/or workstation setups. The reader is advised to consult Haverkort [12] and Fukuda [10] for a detailed discussion on the state space explosion problem.

Linux 2.6 I/O Stack & RAID Subsystems

The I/O scheduler in Linux forms the interface between the generic block layer and the low-level device drivers [2],[4],[8]. The block layer provides functions that are utilized by the file systems and the virtual memory manager to submit I/O requests to block devices (see Figure 1). These requests are transformed by the I/O scheduler and made available to the low-level device drivers. The device drivers consume the transformed requests and forward them (by using device specific protocols) to the actual device controllers that perform the I/O operations. As prioritized resource management seeks to regulate the use of a disk subsystem by an application, the I/O scheduler is considered an imperative kernel component in the Linux I/O path. It is further possible to regulate the disk usage in the kernel layers above and below the I/O scheduler. Adjusting the I/O pattern generated by the file system or the virtual memory manager (VMM) is considered as an option. Another option is to adjust the way specific device drivers or device controllers consume and manipulate the I/O requests. The various Linux 2.6 I/O schedulers can be abstracted into a rather generic I/O model [4],[13].

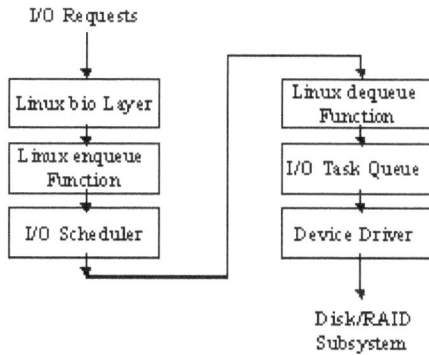

Figure 11-1: Linux 2.6 I/O Stack

The I/O requests are generated by the block layer on behalf of threads that are accessing various file systems, threads that are performing raw I/O, or are generated by virtual memory management (VMM) components of the kernel such as the *kswapd* or the *pdflush* threads. The producers of I/O requests initiate a call to *__make_request()*, which invokes various I/O scheduler functions such as *elevator_merge_fn()*. The *enqueue* functions in the I/O framework intend to merge the newly submitted block I/O unit (a *bio*) with previously submitted requests, and to sort (or sometimes just insert) the request into one or more internal I/O queues. As a unit, the internal queues form a single logical queue that is associated with each block device. At a later stage, the low-level device driver calls the generic kernel function *elv_next_request()* to obtain the next request from the logical queue. The *elv_next_request()* call interacts with the I/O scheduler's dequeue function *elevator_next_req_fn()*, and the latter has an opportunity to select the appropriate request from one of the internal queues. The device driver processes the request by converting the

I/O submission into scatter-gather lists and protocol-specific commands that are submitted to the device controller. From an I/O scheduler perspective, the block layer is considered as the producer of I/O requests and the device drivers are labeled as the actual consumers.

From a generic perspective, every *read()* or *write()* request launched by an application results in either utilizing the respective I/O system calls, or in memory mapping (*mmap*) the file into a process's address space [19]. I/O operations normally result in allocating *PAGE_SIZE* units of physical memory. These pages are being indexed, as this enables the system to later on locate the page in the buffer cache [19]. A cache subsystem though only improves performance if the data in the cache is being reused. Further, the read cache abstraction allows the system to implement read-ahead functionality's, as well as to construct large contiguous (SCSI) I/O commands that can be served via a single direct memory access (DMA) operation. In circumstances where the cache represents pure (memory bus) overhead, I/O features such as direct I/O should be explored (especially in situations where the system is CPU bound). In a general *write()* scenario, the system is not necessarily concerned with the previous content of a file, as a *write()* operation normally results in overwriting the contents in the first place. Therefore, the write cache emphasizes other aspects such as asynchronous updates, as well as the possibility of omitting some write requests in the case where multiple *write()* operations into the cache subsystem result in a single I/O operation to a physical disk. Such a scenario may occur in an environment where updates to the same (or a similar) inode offset are being processed within a rather short time-span. The representation of the block I/O layer in Linux 2.6 encourages large I/O operations. The block I/O layer tracks data buffers by using *struct page* pointers. Linux 2.6 utilizes logical pages attached to inodes to flush dirty data, which allows multiple pages that belong to the same inode to be coalesced into a single *bio* that can be submitted to the I/O layer [2],[4]. This approach represents a process that works well if the file is not fragmented on disk.

The Deadline I/O Scheduler

The deadline I/O scheduler incorporates a per-request expiration-based approach and operates on 5 I/O queues [3],[4]. The basic idea behind the implementation is to aggressively reorder requests to improve I/O performance while simultaneously ensuring that no I/O request is being starved. More specifically, the scheduler introduces the notion of a per-request deadline, which is used to assign a higher preference to *read()* than *write()* requests.

The scheduler maintains the 5 I/O queues. During the *enqueue* phase, each I/O request gets associated with a deadline, and is being inserted in I/O queues that are either organized by the starting logical block number (a sorted list) or by the deadline factor (a FIFO list). The scheduler incorporates separate sort and FIFO lists for *read()* and *write()* requests, respectively. The 5th I/O queue contains the requests that are to be handed off to the device driver. During a dequeue operation, in the case where the dispatch queue is empty, requests are moved from one of the 4 (sort or FIFO) I/O lists in batches. The next step consists of passing the head request on the dispatch queue to the device driver (this scenario also holds true in the case that the dispatch-queue is not empty). The logic behind moving the I/O requests from either the sort or the FIFO lists is based on the scheduler's goal to ensure that each *read()* request is processed by its effective deadline, without starving the queued-up *write()* requests. In this design, the goal of economizing the disk seek time is accomplished by moving a larger batch of requests from the sort list (logical block number sorted), and balancing it with a controlled number of requests from the FIFO list. Hence, the ramification is that the deadline I/O scheduler effectively emphasizes average *read()* request response time over disk utilization and total average I/O request response time.

The Anticipatory I/O scheduler

The anticipatory (AS) I/O scheduler's design attempts to reduce the per thread read response time. It introduces a controlled delay component into the dispatching equation [14],[17],[20]. The delay is being invoked on any new *read()* request to the device driver, thereby allowing a thread that just finished its *read()* I/O request to submit a new *read()* request, basically enhancing the chances (based on locality) that this scheduling behavior will result in smaller seek operations. The tradeoff between reduced seeks and decreased disk utilization (due to the additional delay factor in dispatching a request) is managed by utilizing an actual *cost-benefit* analysis [14]. More specifically, the Linux 2.6 implementation of the anticipatory I/O scheduler follows the basic idea that if the disk drive just operated on a *read()* request, the assumption can be made that there is another *read()* request in the pipeline, and hence it is worth the while to wait [20]. The I/O scheduler starts a timer, and at this point, there are no more I/O requests passed down to the device driver. If a (close) *read()* request arrives during the wait time, it is serviced immediately and in the process, the actual distance that the kernel considers as *close* grows as time passes (the adaptive part of the heuristic). Eventually the *close* requests will dry out and the scheduler will decide to submit some of the *write()* requests.

The CFQ Scheduler

The Completely Fair Queuing (CFQ) I/O scheduler is considered an extension to the better known Stochastic Fair Queuing (SFQ) implementation [18]. The focus of both implementations is on the concept of *fair allocation of I/O bandwidth* among all the *initiators of I/O requests*. An SFQ-based scheduler design was initially proposed (and ultimately being implemented) for some network scheduling related subsystems. The goal to accomplish is to distribute the available I/O bandwidth as equally as possible among the I/O requests. The implementation utilizes n (normally 64) internal I/O queues, as well as a single I/O dispatch queue. During an *enqueue* operation, the PID of the currently running process (the actual I/O request producer) is utilized to select one of the internal queues (normally hash based) and hence, the request is basically inserted into one of the queues (in FIFO order). During dequeue, the SFQ design calls for a round-robin based scan through the non-empty I/O queues, and basically selects requests from the head of the queues. To avoid encountering too many seek operations, an entire round of requests is collected, sorted, and ultimately merged into the dispatch queue. In a next step, the head request in the dispatch queue is passed to the device driver. Conceptually, a CFQ implementation does not utilize a hash function. Therefore, each I/O process gets an internal queue assigned (which implies that the number of I/O processes determines the number of internal queues). In Linux 2.6.5, the CFQ I/O scheduler utilizes a hash function (and a certain amount of request queues) and therefore resembles an SFQ implementation. The CFQ, as well as the SFQ implementations strives to manage per-process I/O bandwidth, and provide fairness at the level of process granularity.

The Noop I/O scheduler

The Linux 2.6 noop I/O scheduler can be considered as a rather minimal-overhead I/O scheduler that performs and provides basic merging and sorting functionality's. The main usage of the noop scheduler revolves around non disk-based block devices (such as memory devices), as well as specialized software or hardware environments that incorporate their own I/O scheduling and (large) caching functionality, and therefore require only minimal assistance from the kernel. Therefore, in large I/O subsystems that incorporate RAID controllers and a vast number of contemporary physical disk drives (TCQ drives), the noop scheduler has the potential to outperform the other 3 I/O schedulers as the workload increases [13].

Modeled I/O Stack

The infrastructure being simulated and analyzed consists of the memory subsystem, a RAID controller with a cache module, and a 4 disk RAID-0 setup. The request coalescing scenarios in the I/O stack are incorporated at the appropriate levels in the model. The workload consists of *read()* and *write()* requests, that depending on the I/O scenario, may be launched in either a sequential or concurrent manner. Based on the I/O scheduler utilized in the simulation, *read()* requests may be favored over *write()* requests [20]. The focus is on evaluating relative I/O performance by incorporating a variety of caching scenarios at the RAID and the disk layers, and by addressing different RAID techniques. More specifically, one major aspect of the study is focused on the write-back verses the write-through RAID cache performance behavior [24]. The 2 caching strategies were implemented in separate models to allow a comprehensive head-to-head comparison. In the write-through *write()* scenario, the data is written to the RAID cache as well as to the physical disk subsystem. The *read()* request are serviced either via the RAID cache (on a cache hit) or the disk subsystem abstraction, respectively.

In the case that the disk subsystem has to be consulted (reflecting a *read()* cache miss scenario), the RAID cache subsystem is updated accordingly. The write-back *write()* scenario consists of writing the data into the RAID cache if ample cache space is available. If the RAID cache is saturated, and hence contains data that has to be flushed out to the disk subsystem, the application *write()* request consists of the following 2 steps. First, a RAID cache *write()* to the disk subsystem to free up some RAID cache space and second, the actual *write()* to the RAID cache. In a *read()* scenario, the request may hit in the RAID cache and simply return. On a cache miss, the *read()* may require either a single *read()* operation from disk (if cache space is available), or may result in (1), a *write()* operation to the disk subsystem to free up some space and (2), a *read()* operation from disk to update the RAID cache subsystem. The possible state-transition behavior of the write-back framework for the *read()* operations is depicted in Figure 2.

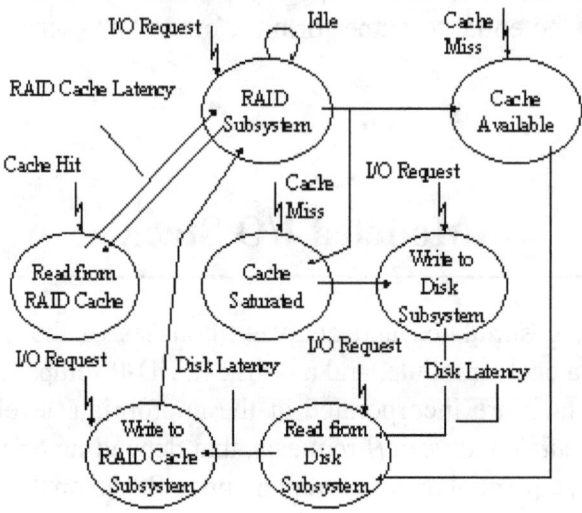

Figure 11-2: Write-Back Cache *read()* Scenarios

DSPN Model

This chapter augments on a vast variety of Petri Net based research studies conducted by Lindemann [16], Antal [1], Ciardo [7], Debes [9], Greiner [11], Bradely [6], Bolch [5], and Kounev [15]. While some of these studies [1],[6],[9],[16] discuss and elaborate on certain systems performance aspects utilizing PN's, the I/O performance of an entire I/O stack under varying workload conditions has not been specifically addressed. The research conducted by Antal [1] revolves around single disk I/O performance under different caching scenarios, and therefore reflects the closest affiliation to this study. From a model implementation perspective, the methodology chosen for this chapter reflects a divide and concur based approach. More specifically, the first phase consisted of implementing a conceptional abstraction model of the Linux 2.6 I/O stack, whereas the second phase, by deduction, augmented on this infrastructure with fine-grain models (smaller state space) hat represent the components that impact I/O performance.

As already discussed, two separate models for the write-back and the write-through caching techniques were implemented. The discussed approach allows (1) evaluating performance, as well as (2) conducting sensitivity studies at various levels of complexity, reflecting either the big I/O picture or the performance behavior of certain low-level components in the I/O stack. Figure 6 in the Appendix depicts the conceptional abstraction model of the entire Linux 2.6 I/O stack, highlighting the possible cache hit behaviors on a main memory and I/O subsystem level. The worst case performance behavior is represented via the I/O path that traverses the entire model from the CPU abstraction down to the actual physical disk drives. Figure 7 (Appendix A) discusses the conceptional setup of a 4-disk RAID system, focusing on the potential performance delta between *read()* and *write()* requests. The model was utilized extensively while evaluating random I/O operations where the I/O request size was equal or less than the strip unit size. Figure 8 (Appendix A) depicts the conceptional abstraction of the Linux 2.6 I/O framework, emphasizing the request coalescing behavior at the bio layer and the I/O scheduler dynamics where the *read()* requests are prioritized over the *write()* requests. Hence, the conceptional abstraction in Figure 8 (Appendix A) reflects the generic behavior of the AS and the deadline schedulers, respectively. Further, the study focused on the traditional behavior of the write-back and write-through cache subsystems, and ignored any additional performance enhancement techniques that may be embedded into contemporary RAID solutions [21],[24].

In this chapter, the actual time parameters of the DSPN models [1] were initialized to express the performance delta among the main memory, the RAID cache, and the disk subsystems, respectively. The next few paragraphs discuss the scenario where the system encounters a main memory cache miss, which results in accessing the RAID and (potentially) the disk subsystems. The workload definition above implies that the Linux I/O infrastructure, more specifically the *bio* and the scheduler layers, has to be traversed in order to process the I/O request. The RAID cache, the disk cache, the disk *read()*, and the disk *write()* access operations were allotted with time units of 1, 10, 100, and 105, respectively. The slight performance delta between the disk *read()* and *write()* operations is due to the fact that the disk drive can initiate a *read()* operation shortly before positioning the read-write heads (in-flight operation) [22]. On the other hand, in the case of a *write()* request, the position of the read-write heads has to precisely match the corresponding sector prior to initiating the physical I/O operation.

Simulation Experiments and Analysis

To reiterate, the goal of this chapter was not to determine effective performance, but rather to quantify the relative performance behavior under different workload and caching scenarios. The firing delays in the DSPN models are either deterministic or exponentially distributed, and were basically initialized utilizing the above discussed performance ratios. The conducted experiments focused on sensitivity studies conducted in a steady-state environment (the models allow transient based studies as well). To establish a performance baseline, the first experiment revolved around random I/O operations and the noop I/O scheduler, simulating a write-back and a write-through RAID cache setup, respectively. The goal of the first simulation study was to establish the asymptotic lower bound (the performance potential) of the I/O subsystem. To simplify the analysis, on a per disk level, the first study only differentiated between a cache hit and a cache miss scenario. The different workload and caching scenarios were simulated via adjusting the firing priorities in the DSPN [1],[25]. The *read()* or *write()* operations were simulated in a loop, which allowed the system to enter a steady state, and to determine the average latency as the reciprocal of the measured throughput. Table 1 summarizes the results (*wt = write-through, wb = write-back*):

Table 11-1 – Random *read()* or *write()* Operations

I/O	Scenario	Time
write	wt, write to disk platter	122
write	wt, write to disk cache	16
write	wb, RAID cache hit	5
write	wb, miss, RAID cache full, disk cache hit	22
write	wb, miss, RAID cache full, write to disk	124
write	wb, miss, RAID cache available	6
read	wt, RAID cache hit	5
read	wt, RAID cache miss, disk cache hit	17
read	wt, read from disk platter	118
read	wb, RAID cache hit	5
read	wb, RAID miss, disk hit, RAID cache free	34
read	wb, RAID miss, disk hit, RAID cache full	142
read	wb, read from disk, RAID cache full	268
read	wb, read from disk, RAID cache free	119

The assumptions made for the first set of experiments are that the average request completion time has a correlation to (1), the state of the RAID and disk cache subsystems and (2), to the probability of locating the data in the respective cache subsystems. The state of the cache subsystems reflects if there is ample space available or not. In the case that either cache subsystem is saturated, some data has to be moved out prior to processing the actual I/O request. In reality, for any given I/O scenario, the cache state, as well as the cache hit behavior are related entities that depend on the locality of the data and the size of the cache subsystems [1],[21],[24]. Table 1 highlights that the write-back *read()* request that encounters a saturated RAID cache subsystem and a disk miss behavior (268 time units) is the most expensive I/O operation.

In this scenario, the physical disk has to be accessed twice, (1) to free some RAID cache and (2), to process the actual *read()* request. Further, the slight performance delta between the *write()* requests to disk in a write-back (124 time units) verses a write-through (118 time units) environment can be explained with the additional overhead caused by determining (in a write-back environment) if the RAID cache contains ample space. As elaborated in Antal [1], Wong [22], and Varki [21], to emphasize the correlation of the cache state and the cache hit behavior, it is feasible at this stage of the study to analyze the *write()* latency behavior under a variety of workload conditions, focusing on the different RAID technologies (see Figure 3).

The workload used in this experiment consisted of *write()* operations that either overwrite certain sections of a file (potential cache hit) or append data to an existing file (cache miss). The DSPN models utilized were configured to reflect the noop I/O scheduler. The cache-hit rate (overwrite verses append ratio) was varied to simulate different I/O scenarios with a RAID cache subsystem that was saturated to 90%. Based on the already discussed design specifications of a write-through architecture, the latency of the write benchmarks did not significantly oscillate in this scenario, and basically stabilized at around 120 time units. The performance behavior of the write-back architecture though was significantly impacted by the cache-hit rate. With ample cache space and a workload specification that did not exceed the size of the RAID cache, the write-back cache executed the benchmark at RAID cache speed at the 100% hit rate. While decreasing the cache hit rate (and hence increasing the number of append operations), the latency increased up to the point where the write-back cache provided a slightly worse average latency than the write-through architecture. Therefore, in more general terms, as the hit rate of the write-back cache decreases, the dependency of the latency behavior to the cache saturation level increases.

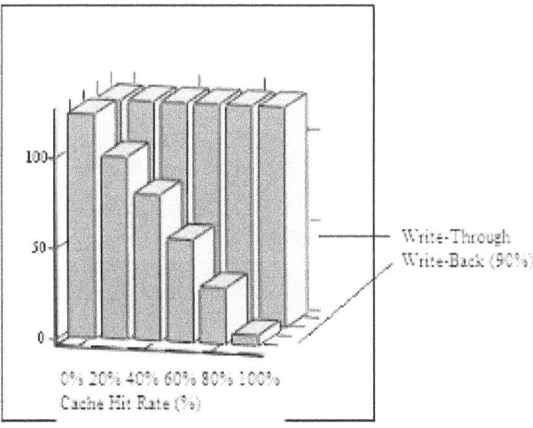

Figure 11-3: I/O *write()* Performance (Latency in Time Units)

The next two experiments conducted for this study revolve around a heterogeneous workload pattern consisting of 50% random *read()* and 50% random *write()* operations. As in the previous experiment, the study varied the cache hit rate and benchmarked write-back and write-through RAID cache systems that were saturated to 10%, 50%, and 90%, respectively. Further, the focus was on determining any potential performance delta between the Linux 2.6 AS and noop schedulers (Figure 4 & Figure 5), respectively. In both experiments, the latency is expressed as generic time units, as the focus is on comparing the relative performance of the different I/O subsystems.

In the mixed, noop based workload scenario, as the cache hit rate decreases (and as the space available in the cache subsystem reflects a scarce resource), the write-through technology is capable of outperforming the write-back architecture (Figure 4). The additional status operations necessary in the write-back implementation, as well as the already discussed performance issues surrounding a saturated write-back architecture contribute to the observed I/O behavior.

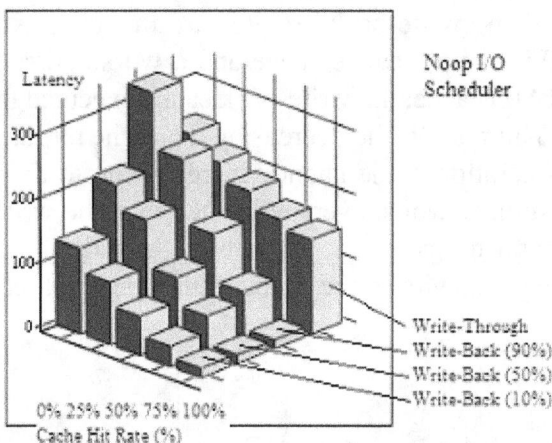

Figure 11-4: Mixed Workload (Noop)

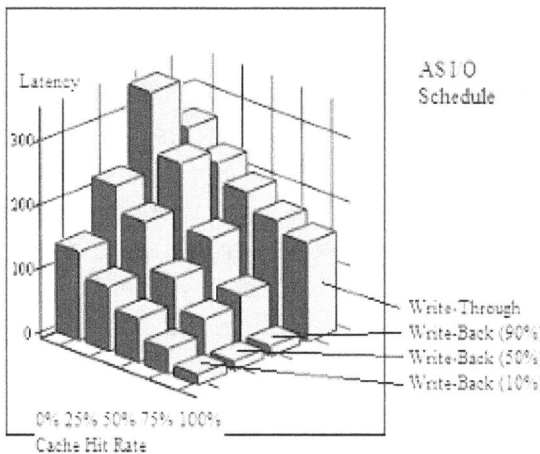

Figure 11-5: Mixed Workload (AS)

Basically the same (relative) performance behavior as with the noop I/O scheduler is reflected in an AS based infrastructure. From an I/O scheduler perspective, based on the simulated random I/O workload and the set of benchmarked data points, the noop scheduler was able to outperform AS by approximately 5% (measured in average relative time units). As the AS scheduler design focuses on preventing *deceptive idleness* [14], and decides to prioritizes the *read()* over the *write()* requests, the random workload mix simulated in this experiment hampers the throughput potential of the AS scheduler. The random/ mixed workload results observed in this study were confirmed via an empirical analysis that was executed on a Linux 2.6 SMP system, using a RAID-0 setup and the xfs file system as the I/O framework. The actual benchmark results revealed a similar I/O pattern (behavior), where the noop scheduler was capable of outperforming AS in a random workload environment.

Summary

The DSPN models presented in this chapter allow quantifying relative performance in a Linux 2.6 centric I/O environment. The proposed models not only focus on some RAID specific components (write-through verses write-back architectures) of the I/O subsystem, but also incorporate the actual memory behavior, as well as some of the optimization techniques imbedded in the Linux 2.6 operating system into the analysis. More specifically, the DSPN's quantify the performance behavior of the *bio* layer and the Linux 2.6 I/O schedulers, incorporating potential request coalescing, request re-ordering, and request prioritizing scenarios into the performance equation. The computational efficiency of the presented models allows conducting sensitivity studies (focusing on relative performance) in a fraction of the time necessary to execute an empirical analysis. The main challenge in this project was to decompose the I/O stack, and hence generate individual DSPN's that represent a state space complexity that was reasonable and manageable for the resources at hand. The insights gained via the DSPN I/O models were utilized in some additional studies to improve the actual performance and scalability of the Linux 2.6 operating system.

References

1.   Antal, B., Bondavalli, A., Somoncini, L., "Reachability and Timing Analysis in Data Flow Networks", CNUCE-CNR, 1996

2.   Arcangeli, A., "Evolution of Linux Towards Clustering", EFD R&D Clamart, 2003

3.   Axboe, J., "Deadline I/O Scheduler Tunables", SuSE, EDF R&D, 2003

4.   Axboe, J., "Linux Block I/O Layer – Present & Future", OLS 04, Ottawa, 2004

5.   Bolch, G., Bruzsa, C., Sztrik, J., "Modeling and Simulation of Markov Modulated Multiprocessor Systems with Petri Nets", University of Erlangen, 1994

6.   Bradley, J., Dingle, N., Harrison, P., Knottenbelt, W., "Performance Queries on Semi Markov Stochastic Petri Nets with an Extended Continuos Stochastic Logic", Imperial College, London, 2003

7.   Ciardo, G., German, R., Lindemann, C., "A Characterization of the Stochastic Process Underlying a Stochastic Petri Net", DAAD, BMFT, 1995

8.   Corbet, J., "Porting drivers to the 2.5 kernel", Linux Symposium, Ottawa, Canada, 2003

9.   Debes, E., "A new Petri Net Based Model of Data Transfer", Swiss Federal Institute of Technology", 1998

10.   Fukuda, H., "On Reduction of State Spaces of Timed Petri Nets", Japan Advanced Institute of Science and Technology, 1996

11.   Greiner, S., Bolch, G., Puliafito, A., Trivedi, K., "Performance Evaluation of Dynamic Priority Operating Systems", Duke University, 1995

12.   Haverkort, B., Moorsel, A., "Using the Probabilistic Evaluation Tool for the Analytical Solution of Large Markov Models", University of Twente, University of Illinois, 1996

13.   Heger, D., Pratt, S., "Workload Dependent Performance Evaluation of the Linux 2.6 I/O Schedulers", OLS 04, Ottawa, 2004

14.   Iyer, S., Drushel, P., "Anticipatory Scheduling – A disk scheduling framework to overcome deceptive idleness in synchronous I/O", SOSP 2001

15.   Kounev, S., Buchmann, A., "Performance Modeling of Distributed E-Business Applications using Queueing Petri Nets", University of Darmstadt, 2003

16.   Lindemann, C., Reuys, A., "Modeling Web Proxy Cache Architectures", University of Dortmund, GMD, 2000

17.   Nagar, S., Franke, H., Choi, J., Seetharaman, C., Kaplan, S., Singhvi, N., Kashyap, V., Kravetz, M., "Class-Based Prioritized Resource Control in Linux", 2003 Linux Symposium,

18.   McKenney, P., "Stochastic Fairness Queueing", INFOCOM, 1990

19.   Mosberger, D., Eranian, S., "IA-64 Linux Kernel, Design and Implementation", Prentice Hall, NJ, 2002

20.   Piggin, N., "Anticipatory I/O Scheduler", UNIX Source Code Documentation (as-iosched.txt), 2004

21.   Varki, E., Merchant A., Qiu, X., "An Analytical Performance Model of Disk Arrays under Synchronous I/O Workloads", UNH Research, 2001

22.   Wong, B., "Configuration and Capacity Planning for Solaris Servers", Sun Microsystems, 1997

23.   Ye, W., "Modeling and Analysis of Quality of Service", Master Thesis, University of Western Ontario, 2000

24.   Hennessy, J., Patterson, D., "Computer Architecture, a Quantitative Approach", Morgan Kaufmann, Third Edition, 2003

25.   Colombo, A., Saiz, A, "System Modeling with Petri Nets", System Reliability Assessment, pp. 102-143, 1990

26.   Gross, D., Harris, C., "Queuing Theory, Second Edition, Wiley, 1998

Chapter 12 - Quantitative Disk I/O Capacity Performance

Introduction

I/O subsystems are widely being considered as the major performance bottleneck in computer systems. In the past decade, the CPU speed enjoyed a hundred-fold increase, whereas the speed of an individual disk drive increased by less than a factor of 10. Many contemporary applications manipulate large amounts of data, and therefore heavily rely on I/O optimization techniques embedded into the operating system, the file systems, and the hardware I/O subsystems, respectively. Parallelization efforts at an application level require a clear understanding of not only the data partitioning scheme employed among multiple (I/O) threads, but also requires quantifying the capacity limits of the underlying storage architecture. As the size and complexity of the operating systems, file systems, user applications, and data files increase, so does the importance of the disk drives capabilities to provide adequate performance. Over the years, magnetic disk drives provided (next to a still significant evolution in processing performance) a new level of complexity to systems design and implantation scenarios. Addressing these issues, this chapter highlights some of the major performance aspects embedded in contemporary disk drives, focusing on disk access optimization techniques incorporated in the software and hardware abstraction layers.

This chapter introduces and elaborates on an analytical I/O performance model that quantifies the expected number of I/O requests to be serviced based on the number of concurrent I/O tasks, disk drives, and the capacity limits of the I/O subsystem. The discussed model is utilized in sensitivity studies to predict workload dependent I/O performance. The argument made throughout the chapter is that the performance prediction for an I/O subsystem is a function of the actual devices in the performance path, and the workload presented to them. Therefore, the focus in this chapter is on developing an analytical I/O model that provides a high level of flexibility, numerical accuracy, and reveals a high degree of prediction power. This chapter was initiated to investigate the possibility of determining a rather simple, efficient, and effective methodology to quantify disk (capacity) performance. Section 1 discusses the current state of contemporary disk technology, focusing on performance and capacity enhancements embedded in the I/O framework. Section 2 introduces the proposed I/O capacity and throughput model, whereas Section 3 elaborates on the simulation and empirical studies conducted to quantify I/O performance in various hardware setups and configuration. The chapter concludes in Section 4 by summarizing the accomplishments and discussing some future work items.

Contemporary Disk Technology

Disk interface protocols such as SCSI, ATA, SAS, or SATA represent the de-facto programming models for disk drives [12],[19]. Earlier disk interfaces only exposed signals to a system, and let the host operating system directly manipulate the drive mechanism and initiate a data transfer. The ramification used to be that the entire set of low-level idiosyncrasies peculiar to disk drives had to be implemented by the firmware's systems software developers [7]. The introduction of the disk interface protocols resulted (1) in migrating the intelligence of maintaining I/O requests from the host system to the disk drives, and (2) in providing a simpler infrastructure to program the use of disk subsystems.

A disk drive is considered as a delivery mechanism for persistent data storage, which utilizes magnetic recording techniques. The design objectives are to provide adequate capacity, reliability, and performance at a minimal cost factor. A single disk drive represents a 3-dimensional space of recorded information. The surface of a disk platter provides 2 dimensions, whereas the stack of disk platters is considered as the third dimension. Adding additional disk platters increases the total capacity in the disk subsystem. This approach though increases the cost factor and causes some difficulties in regards to increasing the disk's *areal density* [1],[2],[15]. Increased vibrations in the spindle, susceptibility to external vibration, and internal disturbance resulting from turbulent airflow are all artifacts of increasing the number of platters in a given space. For decades, drive capacity has been increased by reducing the space between data tracks, measured in tracks per inch (TPI), and increasing the linear density of the bits along a track, measured in bits per inch (BPI). The product of these 2 terms is known as *areal density*, and is measured today in Gbits per square inch. A contemporary disk drive may have 30+ Gbits per square inch. The fact of the matter is that the challenge of designing head, media, and signal-processing systems to achieve higher areal density dominates the development cycle of any disk drive.

In the realm of the older I/O programming model, to locate specific data, the disk drive's logic requires the cylinder, the head, and the sector information. The cylinder specifies the track on which the data resides. Based on the layering technique used, the tracks underneath each other form a cylinder. The head information identifies the specific read-write head, and therefore the exact platter. At this point, the search is narrowed down to a single track on a single platter. Ultimately, the sector value represents the specific sector on the track, and the search is completed. Contemporary disk subsystems do not communicate in terms of cylinders, heads and sectors. Instead, modern disk drives map a unique block number over each cylinder/head/sector construct. Operating systems address the disk drives by utilizing these block numbers (logical block addressing). The culprit is that it is not guaranteed though that the physical mapping is actually sequential [6]. But the statement can be made that there is a rather high probability that a logical block *n* is physically adjacent to a logical block *n+1*. The existence of the discussed sequential layout is paramount to the host system while scheduling or reordering I/O requests. Contemporary disk drives utilize a technology called Zone Bit Recording (sometimes referred to as Zoned Constant Angular Velocity) to increase capacity. Incorporating the technology, cylinders are grouped into zones based on their distance from the center of the disk. Each zone is assigned a number of sectors per track [14]. The outer zones contain more sectors per track compared to the inner zones that are located closer to the spindle. With ZBR disks, the actual data transfer rate varies depending on the physical sector location. Given the fact that a disk drive spins at a constant rate, the outer zones that contain more sectors will transfer data at a higher rate than the inner zones that contain fewer sectors [7].

Performance Implications

One of the most interesting trends in I/O subsystem development revolves around the reduction in the average number of disk platters per drive. Contemporary disk drives utilized in desktop systems are configured with a single platter. A study conducted by Seagate revealed that approximately 31% of the desktop systems in use utilize a single read-write head [2]. These drives demonstrate the impressive increase in areal density over the years, and outline that for the cost sensitive desktop market, a single-disk single-head setup is sufficient to provide the desired cost-performance ratio. The same study concluded that *on average*, disk drives utilized in server and desktop systems use 5 and 2 read-write heads, respectively. Other factors contribute to further reducing the significance of the cylinder dimension. The trend toward smaller diameter disk drives reduces the length of the average tracks and shrinks the size of a typical cylinder. In particular, the highest performance SCSI drives have adopted a smaller diameter media. To illustrate, a 5,400 RPM drive used a 95mm diameter and revealed a seek time of approximately 9ms. A 15,000 RPM drive utilizes a 65mm diameter and provides a seek time of approximately 3.5ms.

More recent changes to the data layout strategies effectively dissolved the cylinder concept. The data blocks used to be arranged on a disk drive so that all sectors in one cylinder were utilized prior to moving to the next cylinder. This concept, which was introduced for performance reasons, may no longer be valid. A newer approach revolves around spiraling the sectors along a single surface (on a per recording zone basis) before moving to another surface in that zone. Sequential access performance may substantially benefit from this new concept [2],[12]. It has to be pointed out though that contemporary disk drives employ different variations of the discussed serpentine format, and that not all disk drives utilize the concept. The ramification though is that the notion of *the cylinder as a fixed location of the actuator* that would be desirable to use as an allocation unit is not necessarily a dependable concept anymore. The introduction of intelligent storage interfaces such as SCSI, ATA, SAS, or SATA boost I/O performance, as these interfaces are capable of buffering data until the host system is ready to process [7],[12],[19]. In a similar fashion, these interfaces can accept data from the host systems without having to first synchronize a host connection to the disk drives. Contemporary disk drives accept a queue of I/O commands. Based on the knowledge of the specific commands, the drive can optimize how the commands are executed and therefore, minimize the time required to complete the set of requests. To illustrate, a contemporary disk drive is capable of executing approximately 170 random I/O requests (with a command queue of 0). This number increases to approximately 320 and 400 with command queues of 32 and 64, respectively [2]. The concept behind command queues is based on the assumption that multiple commands can be issued, and the results can either be buffered in the disk drive or can be returned out of order. The rule of thumb is that the longer the command queue, the greater the possibility to optimize the throughput behavior. It has to be pointed out that the notion of buffering exists in the operating system, the file system, as well as the hardware controllers. Nevertheless, in regards to command queuing, contemporary disk drives provide some significant advantages. To illustrate, this study considers a disk drive that is attached to a single host system. If the host system (software) is managing the I/O queue, the system assumes that the read-write head is positioned at approximately the same location as the last I/O request that was issued. Based on the logical block number, the system will select requests that are close to each other, normally processing commands from one spectrum of the address range to the other one. Utilizing this range of logical block numbers results in submitting a *sequential stream of logical requests* to the I/O subsystem. On the other hand, the disk drive has specific knowledge about the geometry of the data, which is hidden from the host software. The information available to the disk drive includes precise information about the radial track position as well as the angular (or rotational) position of the data. If the disk device supports a command queue, the selection of the next operation is based on the *nearest in time* factor, which may substantially deviate from the logical block number scheme utilized by the host software. The disk drive can take advantage of the seek and rotational distance to generate the optimal set of commands to execute. To reiterate, most contemporary disk drives incorporate on-board command queues that allow a disk device to queue I/O requests locally. The disk controller has the option to reorder the requests in the queue (based on the actual geometry of the data).

The results of these disks access optimization strategies are (1) that the number of transactions per second is maximized and (2) that the order in which the requests are being received is not necessarily the order the requests are getting processed. Thus, the response time of any particular request can not be guaranteed. A request queue may increase spatial locality by selecting requests based on the geometry of the data (which represents a workload transformation), but may also increase the perceived response time because of potential queuing delays (which reflects a behavioral transformation). Therefore, depending on the size of the command queue, an increase in the variation of the response time behavior may occur. To circumvent the issue, the storage interfaces provide a timer construct to determine the maximum time quantity any I/O request can be held before receiving service [12]. In the case that a disk drive services I/O commands from several host systems, the advantages of managing the command queue on a per disk drive level are magnified. To elaborate, 2 host systems may process I/O requests as though each system is the only source of requests. Even if both systems utilize the logical block number paradigm, the conflicts of the 2 independent queues may produce an interference pattern that results in degraded aggregate I/O performance. The disk drive on the other hand can efficiently coalesce the 2 command queues, and therefore operate on a single command queue that is based on the actual geometric layout of the data. In an environment consisting of shared RAID devices, the performance benefits are even more substantial, and therefore noticeable at the user abstraction level.

Disk Capacity & I/O Throughput Model

In a first phase, this study assumes that t I/O threads concurrently request data from a shared I/O subsystem, and hence the statement made is that it is in general impossible for all the I/O requests be serviced simultaneously. This behavior is driven by the fact that the performance limitations of any I/O subsystem introduce an effective upper limit on the number of concurrent I/O requests. In order to service multiple I/O requests, an I/O environment has to be decomposed in d disk drives, each capable of servicing I/O requests independently. In a RAID setup, larger I/O requests may be serviced by a number of successive disk drives. Assuming random I/O (where the request size equals to the stripe unit), the thesis being made is that even if ($t = d$), the full I/O bandwidth can not be utilized by the system. The culprit discussed here is that as t threads issue random I/O requests, it is rather unlikely that the t I/O requests will be serviced by the entire set of disk drives d. The probability that the t I/O requests will be serviced by d disk drives equals to the number of permutations of $\tau(t)$ divided by the number of mappings in $\tau(t)$, where $\tau(t)$ depicts the set of integers *[1 .. t]*. The actual probability (for $t = d$) can be expressed as:

$$P_{d,t} = \frac{t!}{t^t} \quad (1) \qquad \lim_{t \to \infty} \sqrt{\frac{2\pi t}{e^t}} \quad (2)$$

$$x_{d,t} = \sum_{n=1}^{\min(d,\,t)} \frac{n \cdot n! \cdot S(t,n) \binom{d}{n}}{d^t} \quad (3)$$

Equation 2 is further discussed and mathematically elaborated in [9]. One approach to circumvent (or at least alleviate) the performance bottleneck would be to insure that ($d > t$). As the cost of the system increases with every additional disk, the argument made is that it is paramount to understand the correlation among the workload pattern, the I/O bandwidth, and the values of t and d, respectively. Equation based CPU interference models that address a similar issue at the memory level served as one of the discussion baselines for this I/O study [5],[7],[8],[11],[17]. In [8], an equational CPU model was proposed where each processor accesses memory banks with an equal probability. In [17], a model for memory interference on multi-processor system was introduced. In both studies, the memory requests being serviced represent random and independent tasks. The vast research revolving the request interference behavior encountered at the CPU and memory level has only sparsely been discussed at the I/O subsystem level [4],[13]. Based on the discussed research, this study augments on work by Hoogendoorn [8] and Rabinowitz [17], and proposes at this stage a first-order I/O performance model to quantify the expected number of serviced I/O tasks. The model mimics a scenario where each disk d receives multiple requests, but only services a single I/O task. The additional tasks are being rejected (and therefore are not being queued up), basically following the concept of Erlang's loss formula [10]. The number of requests serviced can be expressed as discussed in Equation 3.

In Equation 3, the term $S(t,n)$, the Sterling numbers of the 2nd kind, is further elaborated in [16]. A deficiency of the first order model is the assumption that only 1 I/O request can be serviced per disk drive per I/O cycle. Request coalescing, read-ahead, write-behind, and command queuing techniques employed in contemporary systems therefore justify the introduction of a request parameter r that represents the concurrency factor per I/O cycle. In this chapter, the granularity of an I/O cycle is defined as 1 ms. In other words, the proposed second-order I/O model assumes that each disk drive is capable of servicing r I/O tasks per I/O cycle [3],[20]. The objective of the model is to represent an environment where t independent I/O threads process random requests to d disk drives. Random I/O requests are chosen as the workload pattern, as such a scenario establishes the asymptotic lower bound Ω on I/O performance, circumventing read-ahead and most coalescing efforts in the operating or file systems, respectively.

In other words, evaluating the random I/O performance results in quantifying the (deterministic) I/O capacity behavior that can be sustained by the I/O subsystem. For a single disk drive $d1$, $p(n)$ denotes the probability that the disk drive $d1$ receives n I/O requests. The probability that any I/O request is serviced by a particular disk drive is expressed as $(1/d)$. Hence, the probability that an I/O request will not be serviced by a particular disk drive equals to $(1 - 1/d)$. The objective is to submit n requests to disk $d1$, and therefore all the other I/O requests $(t - n)$ are being serviced by the remaining disk drives in the system. Mathematically, there are $[t\ d]$ possibilities to select t I/O threads to access the disk drive $d1$, or in other words, the requests access $d1$ with a probability equal to $(1/d)^n$. The probability that the I/O requests from the remaining $(t - n)$ I/O threads do not access $d1$ equals to $(1 - 1/d)^{t-n}$. Therefore, the probability $p(n)$, and the expected number of I/O requests $E(d1)$ serviced by the disk drive $d1$, can be defined as outlined in Equations 4 and 5. As only r requests per disk drive can be serviced per I/O cycle, Equation 5 can be mathematically formulated as depicted in Equation 6.

$$p(n) = \binom{t}{n} \left(\frac{1}{d}\right)^{n} \left(1 - \frac{1}{d}\right)^{t-n} \quad (4)$$

$$E_{d1}(d, t) = \sum_{n=0}^{r-1} n \cdot p(n) + \sum_{n=r}^{t} r \cdot p(n) \quad (5)$$

$$E_{d1}(d, t) = \sum_{n=0}^{r-1} n \cdot p(n) + r\left(1 - \sum_{n=0}^{r-1} p(n)\right)$$

$$E_{d1}(d, t) = r + \left[1 - \sum_{n=0}^{r-1} (n - r) \cdot p(n)\right] \quad (6)$$

$$E(d, t) =$$

$$d \cdot r - d\left[\sum_{n=0}^{r-1} (r - n)\left(\frac{1}{d}\right)^{n}\left(1 - \frac{1}{d}\right)^{t-n}\right] \quad \text{of} \quad (7)$$

As the expected number of I/O requests serviced per disk drive is the same, the number of I/O requests serviced (on a per system basis) can be expressed as depicted in Equation 7. The cache-hit factor *(cf),* which is introduced in Equation 7, can be utilized to conduct additional sensitivity studies focusing on a variety of cache behavioral scenarios [7],[13],[20].

Capacity Model Calibration & Validation

The next few paragraphs discuss the potential of the proposed I/O model based on experiments conducted on an 8-way SMP system that was configured with 2GB's of memory, running the Linux 2.6.6 operating system. The I/O subsystem consisted of a RAID controller that was setup with a 2GB-cache, and utilized 5 Seagate ST318452FC disks configured in a RAID-5 environment. While conducting a performance study utilizing a modeling based approach, it is imperative to distinguish between two types of modeling errors, which are referred to as *description* and *prediction* errors, respectively. A description error is defined as the mean relative error among the measured performance indicators of a system (empirical) and the performance indicators of a calibrated model. A description error is only defined inside the range of the actual empirical measurements. On the other hand, the prediction error is defined as the error in predicting the values of performance indicators outside the range of the empirical measurements.

This is a fact that further applies to different configuration setups or varying workload scenario's [6]. Therefore, the 1st phase of the experiment consisted of conducting an empirical analysis where the number of I/O tasks was scaled from 1 to 16. Each I/O thread processed 20,000 4KB random *read()* operations, utilizing a pool of 100,000 files (ranging from 4KB to 64KB) as the benchmark environment. In a 2nd phase, the proposed I/O model was calibrated based on the data gathered via the 1 I/O thread benchmark. Phase 3 consisted of simulating the I/O behavior with up to 16 threads, and to calculate the mean description error. The 4th phase incorporated simulating the I/O behavior with 32 and 64 I/O threads, respectively. The goal was to determine (via empirical runs) the I/O throughput on the system, and ultimately to describe the resulting modeling prediction error.

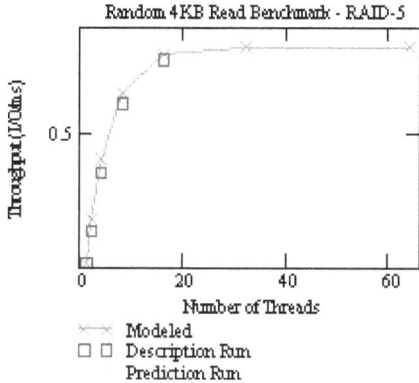

Figure 1: Modeled verses Measured Behavior

Figure 12-1 (graphically) summarizes the conducted experiments. For the random read benchmarks, the aggregated mean description and prediction errors were 5.5% and 4%, respectively. The largest deviation of 10.8% was reported with 2 I/O threads, whereas the smallest error was determined with 16 I/O tasks (2.1%). In general, the best results were obtained with larger I/O thread counts. It is interesting to notice that with up to 16 I/O threads, the model slightly overstated the throughput, whereas with 32 and 64 threads, the model understated the performance by a small margin. It is imperative to note that the simulated trajectory closely captures the I/O behavior determined via the empirical benchmarks, or in other words, the model nicely predicts the asymptotic throughput behavior.

In a second experiment, a sensitivity study was conducted that involved 2 different types of Seagate (ST336752 & ST336607) disk drives, capable of sustaining approximately (estimated) 176 and 146 single-thread random I/O operations, respectively [19]. The model was calibrated to simulate the performance behavior of the 2 drives while scaling the number of disks from 1 to 8, and the number of I/O threads from 1 to 64, respectively.

The analysis revealed that the slower disk reached a throughput of approximately 1,170 I/O operations with 31 threads and 8 disks. Scaling the number of threads beyond 31 threads did not result in any substantial improvement in the I/O throughput behavior, and therefore represents the asymptotic upper bound on the number of threads based on the workload and the resources at hand. For the faster disk scenario, the capacity ceiling at the 8 disk setup was approached with 35 I/O threads, processing approximately 1,407 I/O operations. As expected, the throughput delta between the faster and the slower disk configurations equals to approximately 20%. From an I/O thread perspective, the faster setup reached the asymptotic upper bound with approximately 13% more threads than the slower configuration. The ramification is that the 20% performance shift was achieved with a workload increase (in the number of threads) of only 13%.

Summary

The analytical I/O capacity model presented in this chapter allows quantifying I/O performance with a rather high degree of confidence. The mean error rates obtained across all the benchmarked I/O profiles reflect very encouraging results. The sensitivity study conducted utilizing different disk types reveal the potential of the proposed approach, and outline the flexibility provided by the equation based model. The computational efficiency of the presented model allows conducting sensitivity studies in a fraction of the time necessary to execute an empirical analysis.

As discussed, the disk drive industry is facing some mounting challenges of its own. In recent years, the annual compound growth rate of the disk drive's areal density has been 100% [15]. This growth rate is faster than Moore's Law [7], and therefore the statement can be made that advances in disk technology have outpaced advances in the semiconductor technology. Part of the reason for the rather spectacular growth rate is that the areal density reflects a 2-dimensional challenge. Newer disk drives increase both, the number of tracks per inch from a radial, and the number of linear bits per inch from a circumference perspective. However, both parameters are facing technical challenges that may slow the growth rate.

Conceptually, there are 3 areas where improvements can increase the linear bit density [7],[15]. (1) Disk read-write heads and magnetic media, (2) signal processing in the read channel, and (3) the error correction coding of the disk blocks. Improvements to the read-write heads and the media could deliver the same signal-to-noise ratio (SNR) at an increased BPI. Improved signal processing could deliver the same bit error rate (BER) with a worse SNR. However, the sector error rate can not increase, as it reflects the unrecoverable error rate experienced by the system, and therefore has to be maintained or improved. Improved error correction could deliver the same sector error rate (SER) with a worse BER. In practice, continuous improvements in all 3 areas boosted the growth spurt in disk capacity. In the lights of addressing this challenge, proposals have been made to increase the disk sector size to 4,096 bytes [18]. This is a far-reaching endeavor, as it reflects a user visible change to the disk drive technology. The atomic unit for *write()* requests would be 4,096 bytes.

It has to be pointed out though that larger disk sectors result in boosting the areal density. Applying it to a larger block increases the power of an error-correcting code (ECC). The improved ECC power allows a higher bit error rate, which allows a lower signal-to-noise ratio, which allows for a higher linear bit density for a given disk drive. Longer sectors amortize the per sector overhead over more data, increasing the track format efficiency. An actual implementation of larger sector sizes would require significant operating system and software adjustments though that are still being elaborated, evaluated, and discussed in the industry.

References

1. Anderson, D., "A Drive Perspective", IEEE MMST 03, San Diego, CA, 2003

2. Anderson, D., "From Storage", Storage Journal, Vol. 1, No.4, Seagate Technology, 2003

3. Baired, L., "Definition of Interference and Localization", ISIC 96, 1996

4. Barve, R., Shriver, E., Gibbons, P., Hillyer, B., Matias, Y., Vitter, J., "Modeling and Optimizing I/O Throughput of Multiple Disks on a Bus", Bell Labs, 2000

5. Chang, D., Kuck, D., Lawrie, D., "On the Effective Bandwidth of Parallel Memories" IEEE Transactions on Computers, 1977

6. Ganger, G., Patt, Y., "Using System-Level Models to Evaluate I/O Subsystem Designs", IEEE Computer Society, 1998

7. Hennessy, J., Patterson, D., "Computer Architecture, a Quantitative Approach", Third Edition, Morgan Kaufmann, 2003

8. Hoogendoorn, C., "A General Model for Memory Interference in Multiprocessors," IEEE Transactions on Computers, 1977

9. Impens, C., "Stirling's Series For n!", Pure Mathematics and Computer Algebra, University of Ghent, 2000

10. Jain, R., "The Art of Computer System Performance Analysis", John Wiley, 1991

11. Patel, J., "Analysis of Multiprocessor with Private Cache Memories," IEEE Transactions on Computers, 1982

12.	Riedle, E., Dykes, J., Anderson, D., "ATA vs. SCSI – More Than an Interface", FAST 03, 2003

13.	Shriver, E., Merchant, A., Wilkes, J., "An Analytic Behavior Model with Readahead Caches and Request Reordering", Bell Labs, 1998

14.	Worthington, B., Ganger, G., "Scheduling Algorithms for Modern Disk Drives", ACM Sigmet-Rics Conference, Nashville, TN, May 1994

15.	McCarthy, S., Leis, M., Byan, S., "Large Disk Blocks – Or Not", USENIX 02, Santa Cruz, 2002

16.	Lengyel, T., Gessel, I., "On the Order of Sterling Numbers and Alternating Binomial Coefficient Sums", Brandeis, 1999

17.	Rabinowitz, S., "A Model For Memory Interference in Multi-Processors", Alliant CS, Littleton, MA, 1988

18.	Colegrove, D., "Large Physical Sector Size Proposal", IBM Corporation, 2002

19.	HP, "Workstation Local Disk Technology", Hewlett-Packard Technical White Paper, Palo Alto, CA, 2003

20.	Heger, D., "Modeling and Predicting Load-Dependent I/O Performance in a ZBR Environment", CMG Journal, Issue 111, Summer Edition, 2003

Chapter 13 - An Introduction to Operations Research

Introduction

The term Operations Research (OR) describes the discipline that is focused on the application of information technology for informed decision-making. In other words, OR represents the study of optimal resource allocation. The goal of OR is to provide rational bases for decision making by seeking to understand and structure complex situations, and to utilize this understanding to predict system behavior and improve system performance. Much of the actual work is conducted by using analytical and numerical techniques to develop and manipulate mathematical models of organizational systems that are composed of people, machines, and procedures. This article introduces some of the methods and application that are affiliated with OR, and elaborates on some of the benefits that may be gained by incorporating OR into the actual business framework.

OR Activities

OR's role in both, the public and the private sectors is increasing rapidly. In general, OR addresses a wide variety of issues in transportation, inventory planning, production planning, communication operations, computer operations, financial assets, risk management, revenue management, and many other fields where improving business productivity is paramount. In the public sector, OR studies may focus on energy policy, defense, health care, water resource planning, design and operation of urban emergency systems, or criminal justice. To reiterate, OR reflects an analytical method of problem solving and decision-making that is useful in the management of organizations. In OR, problems are (1) decomposed into basic components and (2) solved via mathematical analysis. Some of the analytical methods used in OR include mathematical logic, simulation, network analysis, queuing theory, and game theory [2]. The actual OR process can in general be described via three steps. (1) A set of potential solutions to a problem is identified and developed (the set may be rather large). (2) The alternatives derived in the first step are analyzed, and reduced to a smaller set of solutions (the solutions have to be feasible and workable). (3) The alternatives derived in the second step are subjected to simulated implementation and, if feasible, exposed to an actual analysis in a real-world environment. It has to be pointed out that in the final step, psychology and management sciences often play a rather important role. Generally speaking, OR improves the effectiveness and the efficiency of an institution, hence some of the benefits offered by OR include:

- Decrease Cost or Investment

- Increase Revenue or Return on Investment

- Increase Market Share

- Manage and Reduce Risk

- Improve Quality

- Increase Throughput while Decreasing Delays

- Achieve Improved Utilization form Limited Resources

- Demonstrate Feasibility and Workability

OR Functions and Methods

OR may assist decision-makers in almost any management function. To illustrate, OR supports the key decision making process, allows to solve urgent problems, can be utilized to design improved multi-step operations (processes), setup policies, supports the planning and forecasting steps, and measures actual results. OR can be applied at the non-manager levels as well, as engineers or consumers alike can benefit from the improved and streamlined decision-making process [4],[5].

When first encountered, the methods commonly utilized in OR may seem obscure. Technical labels such as multi-criteria decision analysis, linear and non-linear programming, discrete-event simulation, queuing and stochastic process modeling, conjoint analysis, or neural networking further foster this general impression. Despite the wealth of labels available in the filed of OR, most projects apply one of three broad groups of methods, which may be described as:

- *Simulation methods*, where the goal is to develop simulators that provide the decision-maker with the ability to conduct sensitivity studies to (1) search for improvements, and (2) to test and benchmark the improvement ideas that are being made.

- *Optimization methods*, where the goal is to enable the decision maker to search among possible choices in an efficient and effective manner, in environments where thousands or millions of choices may actually be feasible, or where some of the comparing choices are rather complex. The ultimate goal is to identify and locate the very best choice based on certain criteria's.

- *Data-analysis methods*, where the goal is to aid the decision-maker in detecting actual patterns and inter-connections in the data set. This method is rather useful in numerous applications including forecasting and data mining based business environments.

Within each of the three basic groups, many probabilistic methods provide the ability to assess risk and uncertainty factors.

OR in Manufacturing

As OR has made (over the years) significant contributions in virtually all industries, in almost all managerial and decision-making functions, and at most organizational levels, the list of OR applications is prodigious. Hence, this article focuses in the next few paragraphs on the manufacturing industry, and introduces some of the application where OR is being used.

The term operations in OR may suggests that the manufacturing application category represents the original home of OR. That is not quite accurate, as the name originated from military operations, not business operations. Nevertheless, it is a true statement that OR's successes in contemporary business pervade manufacturing and service operations, logistics, distribution, transportation, and telecommunication [1]. The myriad applications include scheduling, routing, workflow improvements, elimination of bottlenecks, inventory control, business process re-engineering, site selection, or facility and general operational planning. Revenue and supply chain management reflect two growing applications that are distinguished by their use of several OR methods to cover several functions. Revenue management entails first to accurately forecasting the demand, and secondly to adjust the price structure over time to more profitably allocate fixed capacity. Supply chain decisions describe the who, what, when, and where abstractions from purchasing and transporting raw materials and parts, through manufacturing actual products and goods, and finally distributing and delivering the items to the customers. The prime management goal here may be to reduce overall cost while processing customer orders more efficiently than before. The power of utilizing OR methods allows examining this rather complex and convoluted chain in a comprehensive manner, and to search among a vast number of combinations for the resource optimization and allocation strategy that seem most effective, and hence beneficial to the operation [3],[5].

Production Systems

Businesses and organizations frequently face challenging operational problems whose successful solution requires certain expertise in applied statistics, optimization, stochastic modeling, or a combination of these areas. To illustrate, a company may need to design a sampling plan in order to meet specific quality control objectives. In a manufacturing environment, operations that compete for the same resources must be scheduled in a way that deadlines are not violated. The manager of a supermarket must determine how many checkout lines to keep open at various times during the day and evening so that shoppers are not unnecessarily delayed. Or as a final example, the size of the areas reserved for storing work in process at a number of bottleneck stations has to be determined so that a smooth flow of work results, even at the busiest (peak) production times.

The area of operations research that concentrates on real-world operational problems is called production systems. Production systems problems may arise in settings that include, but are not limited to, manufacturing, telecommunications, health-care delivery, facility location and layout, and staffing. The area of production systems presents special challenges for operations researchers. Production problems are operations research problems, hence solving them requires a solid foundation in operations research fundamentals. Additionally, the solution of production systems problems frequently draws on expertise in more than one of the primary areas of operations research, implying that the successful production researcher can not be one-dimensional. Furthermore, production systems problems can not be solved without an in-depth understanding of the real problem, since invoking assumptions that simplify the mathematical structure of the problem may lead to an elegant solution for the wrong problem [2]. Common sense and practical insight are common attributes of successful production planners. At the current time, the filed of OR is extremely dynamic and ever evolving. To name a few of the contemporary (primary) research projects, current work in OR seeks to develop software for material flow analysis and design of flexible manufacturing facilities using pattern recognition and graph theory algorithms. Further, approaches for the design of re-configurable manufacturing systems and progressive automation of discrete manufacturing systems are under development. Additional OR projects focus on the industrial deployment of computer-based methods for assembly line balancing, business process reengineering, capacity planning, pull scheduling, and setup reduction, primarily through the integration of the philosophies of the Theory of Constraints and Lean Manufacturing [6]. Lean Manufacturing reflects a set of tools and methodologies that aims at the continuous elimination of all *waste* in the production process. The main benefits are (1) lower production costs, (2) increased output and (3) shorter production lead times. More specifically, some of the major goals are:

- *Defects and wastage* - Reduce defects and unnecessary physical wastage, including excess use of raw material (inputs), preventable defects, costs associated with reprocessing defective items, and unnecessary product characteristics which are not required by customers

- *Cycle Times* - Reduce manufacturing lead times and production cycle times by reducing waiting times between processing stages, as well as process preparation times and product/model conversion times

- *Inventory levels* - Minimize inventory levels at all stages of production, particularly works-in-progress between production stages. Lower inventories also imply lower working capital requirements

- *Labor productivity* - Improve labor productivity, both by reducing the idle time of workers and ensuring that when workers are working, they are using their effort as productively as possible

- *Utilization of equipment and space* - Use equipment and manufacturing space more efficiently by eliminating bottlenecks and maximizing the rate of production though existing equipment, while minimizing machine downtime

- *Flexibility* - Have the ability to produce a more flexible range of products with minimum changeover costs and changeover time

- *Output* – In regards to reduced cycle times, increased labor productivity and elimination of bottlenecks and machine downtime can be achieved, companies can generally increase the output from their existing facilities

Most of these benefits discussed above lead to lower unit production costs. To illustrate, more effective use of equipment and space leads to lower depreciation costs per unit produced, more effective use of labor results in lower labor costs per unit produced, and lower defects lead to lower cost of goods sold. The key principles describing Lean Manufacturing can be summarized as:

- *Recognition of waste* – The first step is to recognize what does and does not create value from a client's perspective. Any material, process, or feature that is not required for creating value from the client's perspective is waste and should be eliminated. To illustrate, moving materials among workstations is waste as it can potentially be eliminated

- *Standard processes* – Lean requires an implementation of very detailed production guidelines (labeled Standard Work), that clearly state the content, sequence, timing, and outcome of all actions by workers. This eliminates variation in the way that workers perform their job

- *Continuous flow* – Lean usually aims at the implementation of a continuous production flow that is free of bottlenecks, interruption, detours, back-flows or waiting scenarios. When this is successfully implemented, the production cycle time can be reduced significantly

- *Pull-production* – Just-in-Time (JIT), Pull-production aims at producing only what is needed, when it is needed. Production is pulled by the downstream workstation so that each workstation should only produce what is requested by the next workstation (this approach has to be compared to a Push-production)

- *Quality at the Source* – Lean aims at eliminating defects at the source and for quality inspection to be done by the workers as part of the in-line production process

- *Continuous improvement* – Lean requires striving for perfection by continually removing layers of waste (as they are uncovered). This in turn requires a high level of worker involvement in the continuous improvement process.

Time Series Analysis

Time series data often arise when monitoring industrial processes or tracking corporate business metrics. The essential philosophy behind time series analysis methods is that time series analysis accounts for the fact that data points taken over time may have an internal structure (such as auto-correlation, trend, or seasonal variation) that should be accounted for. In general, there are two main goals of time series analysis. First, identifying the nature of the phenomenon represented by the sequence of observations, and second, forecasting (predicting future values of the time series variable). Both of these goals require that the pattern of observed time series data is identified and (more or less formally) described. Once the pattern is established, the analyst can interpret and integrate it with other data. Regardless of the depth of understanding and the validity of the interpretation (theory) of the phenomenon, one can extrapolate the identified pattern to predict future events.

Further, most time series patterns can be described in terms of two basic classes of components: trend and seasonality. The former represents a general systematic linear or (most often) nonlinear component that changes over time and does not repeat, or at least does not repeat within the time range captured by the data (such as a steady plateau followed by a period of exponential growth). The latter may have a formally similar nature (such as a steady plateau followed by a period of exponential growth), however; it repeats itself in systematic intervals over time. Those two general classes of time series components may coexist in real-life data. To illustrate, production output at a company can rapidly grow over the years, but the trend may still follow consistent seasonal patterns (such as 45% of the yearly production are made in November and December, whereas only 4% of the goods are produced in August).

Forecasting

Predicting the future (forecasting) is paramount to success and survival in today's competitive economy. From manufacturing and inventory to pricing and finance, any organization will be better prepared for the future if it has a better understanding today of what may happen tomorrow. Forecasting allows companies to reduce costs. To illustrate, a company may hold fewer inventories, hire fewer people, or build fewer plants if management *knows* what the future holds. Companies may increase revenues by optimizing manufacturing capacity, making better decisions that are closer to the customer base, or by improving the efficiency and productivity of their marketing budget to drive volume and profits. Further, companies may use forecasting to understand the effects of today's activities on future results. For example, a company may predict the effects of promotions, capital investments, or economic shifts. Organizations normally adhere to a variety of forecasting philosophies such as top-down, bottom-up, straight-line, or accelerated (to name a few). While there is no crystal ball, it is paramount to understand the options that are available. In fact, some companies conduct forecasting by utilizing different methods concurrently to verify the results. If forecasts created by different methods cluster around a certain number (the target), confidence normally builds around that figure.

Some organizations launch forecasts from the lowest level. This bottom-up based approach takes individual outlets, and accumulates sales or production through every channel and division, all the way up through the corporate hierarchy. Other companies utilize a top-down based approach. Starting with the highest echelons of the organization, forecasts are decomposed across the various divisions and channels. Each individual forecast project can be tackled by using one or more statistical methods.

Statistical methods

By utilizing a statistical analysis software package (such as MathCad), a company can develop forecasting models. An organization can choose the actual methods based on either the type of data that is available, or by the type of information the business requires. Some of the more popular methods available are:

- Regression analysis, which can predict the outcome of a given key business indicator (the dependent variable) based on the interactions of other related business drivers (the explanatory variables).

- Dynamic regression, a model that is similar to a regression analysis, but normally produces more realistic results, as the method emphasizes the *ripple effects* that the input variables can have on the dependent variable.

- Trend analysis, a method that relies on determining trends in the time series to predict future results.

- Exponential smoothing, a method that uses a weighted average of past and current values, adjusting the weight on current values to account for the effects of fluctuation in the data (such as seasonality). Using an alpha term (in-between 0 and 1) the method allows adjusting the sensitivity of the smoothing effects. This model is often used for large-scale forecasting projects, as it is both robust and easy to apply.

- ARIMA (AutoRegressive Integrated Moving Average), a method that utilizes lags and shifts in the historical data to uncover patterns (such as a moving average or seasonality) and to predict the future.

- Unobserved components models, which represent a combination of regression and time series forecasting techniques. This approach provides the explanatory power of regression with the important dynamic effects of time series models. The analyst builds a regression model, but also includes unobserved time series components (such as trend and seasonality) into the project. The coefficients of the time series components are dynamic (to account for changing trend or seasonality over time).

In general, businesses and organizations that utilize time series analysis-based methods and forecasting are in a better position to make strategic decisions. These institutions are further better positioned to meet (and satisfy) customer needs, adjust to changing business environments, survive in ever changing economic markets, and increase the bottom-line.

Summary

The driving idea behind OR is to collaborate with clients to design and improve operations, make better decisions, solve problems, and advance managerial functions including policy formulation, planning, forecasting, and performance measurement. The goal of OR is to develop information to provide valuable insight and guidance. By utilizing OR methods, the objective is to apply to any given project the most appropriate scientific techniques selected from mathematics, any of the sciences including the social and management sciences, and any branch of engineering, respectively. The work normally entails collecting and analyzing data, creating and testing mathematical models, proposing approaches not previously considered, interpreting information, making recommendations, and aiding at implementing the initiatives that result from the study. Moreover, utilizing OR methods allow to develop and implement software, systems, services, and products related to a clients methods and applications. The systems may include strategic decision-support systems, which play a vital role in many organizations today.

References

1.   Hillier F., and Lieberman G. "Introduction to Operations Research." Holden-Day, 2001

2.   Banks J., Carson II J., and Nelson B. "Discrete-Event System Simulation." Prentice-Hall, 1995

3.   Rardin, R.L., "Optimization in Operations Research." Englewood Cliffs: Prentice Hall, 1998

4.   Taha, H.A., "Operations Research: An Introduction." Englewood Cliffs: Prentice Hall, 2002

5.   Voss, C., Tsikriktsis, N. and Frohlich, M., "Case research in operations management." Inter. J. of Operations and Production Management, 22, 2, 195-219, 2002

6.   Epply, T., "The Lean Manufacturing Handbook," (Assisted by Judy Nagengast), Second Edition, 2004

Index

A

Active Messages 19
AS 157
availability xiii, xv, xvii, xviii, 8, 15, 16, 25, 28, 30, 31, 36, 46, 65, 66, 67, 68, 69, 70, 71, 72, 74, 80, 81, 89, 95, 99, 114, 117, 118, 119

C

CFQ 158
CIFS 32, 33, 57, 58, 59
cluster file systems 15, 31, 33, 48
cohesive systems assurance 65
compute Grid 3
Criticality Analysis 92
cXFS 33

D

data Grid 3
deadline 156, 161
dependability 65, 67, 71, 154
DSPN 86, 151, 154, 160, 161, 163, 165

E

extra-Grids 3, 4

F

Fibre Channel 32, 34, 38, 54, 55, 56, 57, 59, 60, 61, 62

G

GFS 16, 33, 36, 37, 38, 39, 40, 41, 42, 43, 44, 45, 46, 47
Gigabit Ethernet 2, 4, 35, 55, 59
GigE 55
GPFS 15, 16, 33, 34, 35, 36, 44, 49, 53, 139, 140, 143, 144, 146, 148
Grid xiii, xvii, xviii, 1, 2, 3, 4, 5, 7, 8, 9, 10, 11, 12, 13, 53

H

HA 31, 32, 47, 80

I

IEEE v, 13, 26, 49, 50, 51, 62, 76, 96, 104, 129, 148, 182
InfiniBand 4, 35, 53, 54, 55, 56, 62
inspections 98, 106, 114
inter-Grids 3, 5
intra-Grids 3, 4
IPoIB 55

J

Just-in-Time 190

L

Linux v, 11, 35, 36, 37, 41, 44, 45, 58, 76, 145, 146, 151, 152, 154, 155, 156, 157, 158, 160, 161, 164, 165, 167, 168, 178
Lustre 33, 49

M

maintainability xiii, xv, xvii, xviii, 8, 65, 66, 67, 68, 69, 71, 72, 73, 81, 95, 112, 114
Message Passing Interface 20, 55, 133
middle-ware 4, 5, 6, 11, 84
MIMD 17, 21, 133, 136
Moore's Law 180
MPP 17, 22, 24, 25, 131, 133, 139, 140, 143, 146, 147, 148
Myrinet 4

N

NAS xvii, xviii, 45, 53, 56, 57, 58, 59, 61, 145, 146, 149
NFS 32, 33, 57, 58, 59, 62
noop 158, 162, 163, 164, 165
NUMA 18, 22, 25, 26, 27, 29, 30, 49, 131, 133

O

OpenMP 20
Operations Research 66, 185, 196

P

Parallel Virtual Machine 20, 133
predictive maintenance 97, 105, 114
preventive maintenance 97, 98, 101, 103, 105, 106,
    110, 111

R

RAID 56, 113, 114, 139, 144, 151, 152, 154, 158,
    159, 161, 162, 163, 164, 165, 175, 178
RDBMS 19, 132
reliability xiii, xv, xvii, xviii, 8, 24, 28, 65, 66, 67,
    68, 69, 70, 71, 72, 80, 89, 90, 91, 94, 95, 97,
    100, 101, 102, 104, 105, 106, 109, 112, 113,
    114, 118, 172
RPC 19

S

safety 65, 66, 69, 70
SAN xvii, xviii, 15, 31, 32, 33, 34, 35, 36, 37, 44,
    45, 47, 53, 55, 56, 57, 58, 59, 60, 61, 62
scalability v, xiii, xv, xvii, xviii, xix, 8, 15, 23, 24,
    25, 28, 30, 39, 45, 46, 48, 55, 65, 66, 70, 81,
    89, 95, 131, 132, 136, 137, 138, 143, 145,
    146, 166
scaleup function 134, 135, 136, 137, 140, 141, 142,
    146, 147, 148
SCSI 38, 39, 45, 56, 57, 59, 156, 172, 173, 174,
    183
Seagate 173, 178, 179, 182
security xiii, xv, xviii, 3, 4, 9, 10, 11, 58, 65, 66,
    69, 71, 72, 80, 81
Sequence Diagrams 82, 84
SMP xiii, xiv, 16, 17, 20, 24, 25, 26, 27, 29, 30, 55,
    71, 72, 131, 133, 137, 139, 143, 144, 147,
    148, 165, 178
Software Engineering 81
speedup function 132, 134, 135, 136

T

TCP/IP 54, 55, 56, 57, 58
TeraGrid 5

U

UMA 17, 22, 23, 25

UNIX 15, 21, 29, 36, 37, 58, 61, 71, 72, 168

V

VLAN 117, 120, 121, 124, 125, 126, 127
VMM 25, 26, 28, 30, 155